First World War
and Army of Occupation
War Diary
France, Belgium and Germany

58 DIVISION
Divisional Troops
504 Field Company Royal Engineers
25 January 1917 - 28 June 1919

WO95/2996/4

The Naval & Military Press Ltd
www.nmarchive.com
Published in association with The National Archives

Published by

The Naval & Military Press Ltd

Unit 10 Ridgewood Industrial Park,

Uckfield, East Sussex,

TN22 5QE England

Tel: +44 (0) 1825 749494

www.naval-military-press.com

www.nmarchive.com

This diary has been reprinted in facsimile from the original. Any imperfections are inevitably reproduced and the quality may fall short of modern type and cartographic standards.

© **Crown Copyright**
Images reproduced by permission of The National Archives, London, England, 2015.

Contents

Document type	Place/Title	Date From	Date To
Heading	WO95/2996/4		
War Diary	Southampton	25/01/1917	25/01/1917
War Diary	Lehavre	26/01/1917	27/01/1917
War Diary	Monterolier Buchy	27/01/1917	27/01/1917
War Diary	Abbeville	28/01/1917	28/01/1917
War Diary	Frevent	28/01/1917	28/01/1917
War Diary	Beauvior	29/01/1917	29/01/1917
War Diary	Le Souich	29/01/1917	31/01/1917
Heading	War Diary 504 Field Coy RE Vol II		
War Diary	Lesouich	02/02/1917	02/02/1917
War Diary	Bailleulmont	03/02/1917	12/02/1917
War Diary	Le Souich	13/02/1917	13/02/1917
War Diary	Bailleulmont	14/02/1917	15/02/1917
War Diary	Sus-St-Leger	16/02/1917	20/02/1917
War Diary	Souastre	21/02/1917	21/02/1917
War Diary	Henu	22/02/1917	25/02/1917
Heading	War Diary Of 504th Field Coy RE From 26-2-17 To 26-3-17 Volume II		
War Diary	Henu	26/02/1917	27/02/1917
War Diary	Souastre	27/02/1917	27/02/1917
War Diary	Fonquevillers	28/02/1917	01/03/1917
War Diary	Souastre	01/03/1917	01/03/1917
War Diary	Fonquevillers	02/03/1917	02/03/1917
War Diary	Souastre	02/03/1917	07/03/1917
War Diary	Larbret	07/03/1917	10/03/1917
War Diary	Humbercamp	11/03/1917	13/03/1917
War Diary	Pommier	14/03/1917	19/03/1917
War Diary	Ransart	20/03/1917	21/03/1917
War Diary	Pommier	22/03/1917	29/03/1917
War Diary	Lucheux	30/03/1917	31/03/1917
War Diary	Boquemaison	01/04/1917	01/04/1917
War Diary	Laneuville	02/04/1917	04/04/1917
War Diary	Boquemaison	04/04/1917	05/04/1917
War Diary	Monchy Au Bois	06/04/1917	12/04/1917
War Diary	Bus-Les-Artois	13/04/1917	14/04/1917
War Diary	Achiet Le Grand	15/04/1917	17/04/1917
Miscellaneous	A Form Messages And Signals		
War Diary	Achiet Le Grand	18/04/1917	02/05/1917
War Diary	Vaulx Vraucourt	03/05/1917	09/05/1917
War Diary	Lagnicourt	10/05/1917	11/05/1917
War Diary	Vaulx Vraucourt	12/05/1917	18/05/1917
War Diary	Mory	19/05/1917	19/05/1917
War Diary	Bihucourt	19/05/1917	19/05/1917
War Diary	Vaulx-Vraucourt	19/05/1917	25/05/1917
Miscellaneous	O/550th Field Rgt.	18/05/1917	18/05/1917
Miscellaneous	Brig. General Freyberg V.C., D.S.O.	23/05/1917	23/05/1917
Miscellaneous	173rd Infantry Brigade	17/05/1917	17/05/1917
War Diary	Vaulx-Vraucourt	26/05/1917	31/05/1917
Miscellaneous	504 Fd Coy RE Vol 6		
Miscellaneous	On His Majesty's Service.		

War Diary	Vaulx-Vraucourt	01/06/1917	01/06/1917
War Diary	Ervillers	05/06/1917	08/06/1917
Miscellaneous	173rd Infantry Brigade	09/06/1917	09/06/1917
War Diary	Ervillers	09/06/1917	11/06/1917
Miscellaneous	173rd Infantry Brigade Operation Order No. 25	08/06/1917	08/06/1917
Miscellaneous	173rd Artillery Barrage Time Table-Attached Operation Order No. 25		
Miscellaneous	173rd Infantry Brigade	08/06/1917	08/06/1917
Miscellaneous	173rd Infantry Brigade		
Map	Map		
Miscellaneous	173rd Infantry Brigade Operation Order No. 25	10/06/1917	10/06/1917
Miscellaneous	173rd Brigade Amended Barrage Time-Table Attached To Operation Order No. 25		
Miscellaneous	504th Field Coy R.E.		
Miscellaneous	O.C. 504 (Wessex) Field Core	10/06/1917	10/06/1917
War Diary	Ervillers	12/06/1917	14/06/1917
Operation(al) Order(s)	All Recipients Of 173rd Infantry Brigade Operation Order No. 30	14/06/1917	14/06/1917
Miscellaneous	173rd Infantry Brigade Operation Order No. 30	14/06/1917	14/06/1917
Miscellaneous	173rd Brigade Barrage Time Table Attached To Operation Order No:- 30		
Miscellaneous	Secret To All Concerned	14/06/1917	14/06/1917
Miscellaneous	Original Administrative Instructions Issued With Operation Order No. 25	14/06/1917	14/06/1917
Map	Map		
War Diary	Ervillers	14/06/1917	15/06/1917
Operation(al) Order(s)	173rd Infantry Brigade Operation Order No 31	15/06/1917	15/06/1917
Map	Map		
War Diary	Ervillers	15/06/1917	19/06/1917
War Diary	Ablainzevelle	20/06/1917	08/07/1917
War Diary	Bancourt	09/07/1917	09/07/1917
War Diary	Neuville	10/07/1917	12/07/1917
War Diary	Bourjonval	12/07/1917	20/07/1917
Miscellaneous	Operation Order No. 30 by O.C. 504 Field Co RE	15/07/1917	15/07/1917
War Diary	Neuville Bourjonval	21/07/1917	31/07/1917
Miscellaneous	Operation Orders By O.C 504 Field Coy R.E	28/07/1917	28/07/1917
Miscellaneous	Operation Orders By O.C. 504th Field Coy RE	28/07/1917	28/07/1917
War Diary	Fosseux	01/08/1917	03/08/1917
War Diary	Tilloy Lez Mofflains	04/08/1917	14/08/1917
Miscellaneous	C.R.E. 58th Division No I/1475	05/08/1917	05/08/1917
War Diary	Tilloy Lez Mofflains	15/08/1917	24/08/1917
War Diary	Poperinghe	25/08/1917	28/08/1917
War Diary	East Canal Bank	29/08/1917	29/08/1917
War Diary	Ypres	30/08/1917	31/08/1917
Miscellaneous	C.R.E. 58th Division	21/08/1917	21/08/1917
Miscellaneous	Special Order By Maj R. Shockett Cmdg 504 Fd Coy R.E	23/08/1917	23/08/1917
War Diary	East Canal Bank	01/09/1917	12/09/1917
War Diary	East Canal Bank Ypres	13/09/1917	27/09/1917
War Diary	Poperinghe	28/09/1917	28/09/1917
Miscellaneous	XVIII Corps		
Miscellaneous	O.C. 504 Field Coy Re	22/09/1917	22/09/1917
War Diary	Poperinghe	29/09/1917	30/09/1917
War Diary	Louches	01/10/1917	09/10/1917
War Diary	Hospital Farm Camp Ref Sheet 28.N.W. B 19d.3.4	10/10/1917	14/10/1917
War Diary	Hospital Farm Camp Ref. Sheet 28. N.W. B 19.d.3.2	15/10/1917	24/10/1917

War Diary	Murat Farm B30a8.2.	25/10/1917	28/10/1917
Miscellaneous	O.C. 504th Field Coy	02/10/1917	02/10/1917
War Diary	Murat Farm	29/10/1917	06/11/1917
Miscellaneous	173rd Inf Bde.	02/11/1917	02/11/1917
Miscellaneous	O.C. 504th Fd. Co RE	01/11/1917	01/11/1917
War Diary	Murat Farm	07/11/1917	16/11/1917
War Diary	Portland Camp	17/11/1917	25/11/1917
War Diary	Samette	26/11/1917	26/11/1917
War Diary	Colembert	27/11/1917	08/12/1917
War Diary	Samette	09/12/1917	09/12/1917
War Diary	Canal Bank West	10/12/1917	17/01/1918
War Diary	Proven	18/01/1918	21/01/1918
War Diary	Thezy Glimont	22/01/1918	24/01/1918
War Diary	Rosieres	25/01/1918	25/01/1918
War Diary	Roye	26/01/1918	26/01/1918
War Diary	Salency	27/01/1918	27/01/1918
War Diary	Behencourt	28/01/1918	28/01/1918
War Diary	Pierremande	29/01/1918	31/01/1918
War Diary	Buttes De Rouy	25/02/1918	28/02/1918
War Diary	Buttes De Rouy	17/02/1918	24/02/1918
War Diary	Butte De Rouy	11/02/1918	16/02/1918
War Diary	Pierremande	01/02/1918	05/02/1918
War Diary	Les Butte Rouy Map Ref 70 D. NW. H.1.c 8-2	06/02/1918	10/02/1918
War Diary	Sinceny	01/03/1918	24/03/1918
War Diary	Pierre-Mande	25/03/1918	31/03/1918
Heading	War Diary 504th Field Company, R.E April 1918		
War Diary	Pierre-Mande	01/04/1918	05/04/1918
War Diary	Near Cagny	06/04/1918	27/04/1918
War Diary	Coulonvillers	28/04/1918	30/04/1918
Miscellaneous	58th Divn. No.a5/10,020	30/03/1918	30/03/1918
Heading	War Diary Of 504th Field Coy. R.E From 1-5-18 To 31-5-18 Vol 17		
War Diary	Coulonvillers	01/05/1918	07/05/1918
War Diary	Baizieux	08/05/1918	16/05/1918
War Diary	Warloy	16/05/1918	23/05/1918
War Diary	Henencourt Wood	24/05/1918	31/05/1918
Heading	War Diary Of 504th (Wessex) Field Coy RE Period 1-6-18 To 30-6-18 Vol 18		
War Diary	Henencourt Wood	01/06/1918	01/06/1918
War Diary	Bois De Sauville	02/06/1918	04/06/1918
War Diary	Mirvaux	05/06/1918	10/06/1918
War Diary	Saveuse	11/06/1918	16/06/1918
War Diary	Bois De Molliens	17/06/1918	17/06/1918
War Diary	Bois Robert	18/06/1918	18/06/1918
War Diary	Lavienville	19/06/1918	25/06/1918
War Diary	Bois De Robert	26/06/1918	28/06/1918
War Diary	Baizieux	29/06/1918	30/06/1918
Heading	War Diary Of 504th (Wessex) Field Coy R.E. For Period 1-7-18 To 31-7-18 Vol 19		
War Diary	Baizieux	01/07/1918	11/07/1918
War Diary	Lawrence Wood D.19.a.5.0	12/07/1918	18/07/1918
War Diary	Basieux C.5.a.8.4	19/07/1918	28/07/1918
War Diary	Ribemont D.26.b.1.9	29/07/1918	31/07/1918
Heading	504th Field Company Royal Engineers August 1918		
War Diary	Ribemont D.26.b.1.9	01/08/1918	02/08/1918
War Diary	Baslieux	03/08/1918	03/08/1918

War Diary	Berteaucourt	04/08/1918	04/08/1918
War Diary	Bois De Escard Onneuse 62.D NW.I.15.a.9.6	05/08/1918	24/08/1918
War Diary	S. of Morlan-Court K.14.d.3.4	25/08/1918	26/08/1918
War Diary	Cas Valley K.12.b.4.6	27/08/1918	27/08/1918
War Diary	S. of Citadel F.21.d.70	28/08/1918	29/08/1918
War Diary	Billon Wood Valley	30/08/1918	31/08/1918
Heading	War Diary Of 504th (Wessex) Field Coy R.E. (T) For Period 1-9-18 To 30-9-18 Vol 21		
War Diary	Billon Wood Valley A.25.d.6.7	01/09/1918	04/09/1918
War Diary	No. Of Hem	05/09/1918	06/09/1918
War Diary	Bouchesvesnes	07/09/1918	07/09/1918
War Diary	Moislains	07/09/1918	12/09/1918
War Diary	S.E. Of Nurlu	13/09/1918	24/09/1918
War Diary	Montauban	25/09/1918	27/09/1918
War Diary	Lependu	28/09/1918	29/09/1918
War Diary	Bully Grenay	30/09/1918	30/09/1918
Heading	War Diary Of 504th Field Coy RE For Period 1-10-18 To 31-10-18		
War Diary	Bully Grenay	01/10/1918	02/10/1918
War Diary	St. Pierre	03/10/1918	14/10/1918
War Diary	Harnes	15/10/1918	18/10/1918
War Diary	Courrieres	19/10/1918	19/10/1918
War Diary	Sec Mont	20/10/1918	20/10/1918
War Diary	Lannay	20/10/1918	21/10/1918
War Diary	Rongy	22/10/1918	31/10/1918
Heading	War Diary Of 504th Field Company R.E For The Period 1.11.18 To 30.11.18		
War Diary	Rongy	01/11/1918	09/11/1918
War Diary	Bleharies	10/11/1918	10/11/1918
War Diary	Wiers	11/11/1918	11/11/1918
War Diary	Beloeil	12/11/1918	29/11/1918
War Diary	Weirs	30/11/1918	31/12/1918
Miscellaneous	504 Fd Coy RE Vol 25		
War Diary	Wiers	01/01/1919	22/02/1919
War Diary	Leuze	23/02/1919	31/05/1919
Miscellaneous	R.E Records G.H 2	20/06/1919	20/06/1919
War Diary	Leuze	01/06/1919	13/06/1919
War Diary	Antwerp	14/06/1919	16/06/1919
War Diary	Boulogne	17/06/1919	28/06/1919

WO 95/29964

Army Form C. 2118.

Sheet 1

WAR DIARY
or
INTELLIGENCE SUMMARY.
(Erase heading not required.)

Instructions regarding War Diaries and Intelligence Summaries are contained in F. S. Regs., Part II. and the Staff Manual respectively. Title pages will be prepared in manuscript.

504TH FIELD COY. R.E.

Vol I

Place	Date	Hour	Summary of Events and Information	Remarks and references to Appendices
SOUTHAMPTON	25-1-17	14-0	Embarked on S.S. "Siptah" – 3 Officers, 92 other ranks, 51 horses, 27 mules & full equipment of Vehicles	
		17-0	" " S.S. Queen Alexandra – 4 Officers & 120 other ranks (Officer i/c Lieut. Cunningham)	
		18-15	S.S. "Siptah" left.	
		18-30	S.S. Queen Alexandra left.	
LE HAVRE	26-1-17	1-30	S.S. Queen Alexandra disembarked 4 Officers & 120 other ranks – no casualties & proceeded	
			to Halle & Gare Maritime.	
		12-0	S.S. "Siptah" landed 3 Officers, 92 other ranks, 51 horses, 27 mules & full equipment Vehicles	
		15-0	S.S. Siptah cleared & fatigues finished.	
		15-30	Last details of unit arrive at Halle 4, Gare Maritime	
		15-45	Instructions received to proceed with all ranks to Docks Rest camp – leaving Horses & Vehicle at Halle 4 with Guard & Stable Picket.	
		18-15	Arrived Dock Rest Camp & reported to O.C. Received orders to report with unit complete to D.A.D.R.T. Gare du Marchandise at 8.30 hrs on 27-1-16 for entrainment.	
27-1-17		8-0	Left Halle 4 Gare Maritime with unit complete with unit detachment of 1 charger left with A.V.C. company	
		8.20	Arrived Point 3 Gare Marchandise & commenced entraining as directed by officer representing D.A.D.R.T.	
		10.45	Received orders stating my train left at 11.15 hrs.	
		11.15	Train left Le Havre.	
MONTÉROLIER BUCHY		20.40	Train stops for watering horses – hot meals provided for men.	
		21.10	Train left.	

Army Form C. 2118.

Sheet II

WAR DIARY
or
INTELLIGENCE SUMMARY.
(Erase heading not required.)

Instructions regarding War Diaries and Intelligence Summaries are contained in F.S. Regs, Part II. and the Staff Manual respectively. Title pages will be prepared in manuscript.

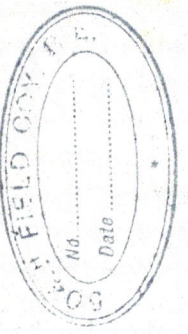

Place	Date	Hour	Summary of Events and Information	Remarks and references to Appendices
ABBEVILLE	28-1-17	5.45	Train arrives - 18 hours late according to schedule. Orders received from R.T.O. to proceed by same train to TREVENT.	
		18.30	Train leaves.	
TREVENT	"	23.0	Train arrives after journey of nearly 36 hrs in extremely cold weather - no casualties. Orders delivered by R.T.O. from H.Q. 17th 3rd Inf. Bde. to proceed to BEAUVOIR. Detraining of own unit & part of Sig. Train commenced.	
BEAUVOIR	29-1-17	2.30	Arrived & commenced detailing billets & arranged by Maire arranged in advance.	
		2.40	Received orders from H.Q. 17th 3rd Inf. Bde. to take place in line of march at 10.35 & proceed to LE SOVICH.	
		10.35	Passed starting point for march to LE SOVICH.	
		11.0	Received verbal instructions to march via BOQUETMAISON.	
LE SOVICH		17.20	Arrived at LE SOVICH having been delayed at BOQUETMAISON by other troops & at level crossing - no casualties.	
	30-1-17		Training by sections - 1 driver sent to Hospital at SUS LE GRAND.	
	31-1-17		Training by sections - 1 driver sent to Hospital at SUS LE GRAND.	

R. J. ??? Maj.
O.C. 504TH FD. COY. R.E.
LE SOVICH

WAR DIARY Vol I

50th FIELD COY. RE

Army Form C. 2118.

WAR DIARY
or
INTELLIGENCE SUMMARY.   504 Fd. Coy. R.E.
(Erase heading not required.)

Place	Date	Hour	Summary of Events and Information	Remarks and references to Appendices
LE SOUICH	Feb 17 2	9.30 a.m.	Orders received from H.Q. 173 Inf. Bde to move at 10.30 a.m. to BAILLEULMONT.	
		10.45	4 officers & 140 O.R. left by Motor Lorry – 1 officer 18 other ranks – 15 horses – 5 vehicles left by road.	
		2.15 pm	Coy arrived BAILLEULMONT & quartered in R.E. Lines 4.9.15 pm.	
			Detail of Coy left at LE SOUICH with Lieut. Cunningham (sick) 2/Lt. Otwe in charge.	
BAILLEULMONT	3		Officers & Senior N.C.Os conducted through Trenches by O.C. 458 Fd. Coy. R.E.	
	4		Coy. employed on Dugout construction & Trench repair & improvement.	
	5		ditto	
	6		ditto	
	7		ditto	
	8		ditto	
	9		ditto	
	10		ditto	
	11		Coy rest day.	
	12		Coy. employed on Dugout Construction & Trench repair & improvement.	
LE SOUICH	13		Detail of Coy. move from LE SOUICH to BUS ST LEGER.	
BAILLEULMONT	14		Coy employed on Dugout Construction & Trench repair. Orders received to move to BUS ST LEGER.	
	15		Coy moved at 9.30 a.m. to BUS ST LEGER.	
BUS ST LEGER	16		Coy. refitting. Information received that Infantry were to be permanently attached to Fd. Coy as pioneers as there would be no Pioneer Battn in the Divn.	
	17	2.1 pm	200 Infantry reported – 50 each from 2/1, 2/2, 2/3 & 2/4 Bn London Regt. Royal Fusiliers. Orders received to move to HENU on 20th. with advanced party to go as soon as furniture.	R.F. Freeman Maj.

WAR DIARY
or
INTELLIGENCE SUMMARY.

Army Form C. 2118.

504 Fd. Coy. R.E.

Place	Date	Hour	Summary of Events and Information	Remarks and references to Appendices
SVS ST LEGER	Feb/17 18	9.30 a.m.	Advanced party left for HENU to take over R.E. workshop there & also to take over R.E. work on line of 3 Field Corps. R.E. of 46 Divn. Party consisted of O.C. & 1st Row & 12 N.C.O.s & men.	
	19		Coy. refitting. Advanced Party taken over at HENU, SOUASTRE, BIENVILLERS, GAUDIEMPRE, BERLES and FONQUEVILLERS.	
	20		Coy. moves to HENU & proceeds thence (less No 4 Section & Details) to SOUASTRE. No 4 Section established at HENU with No 4 Section for R.E. Workshops & Dump. Coy. H.Q.	
SOUASTRE	21		Sections proceed to take up works on line vacated by 3 Fd Corps R.E. 46 Divn. as follows – No 1. Section, FONQUEVILLERS area – No 2. Section, BIENVILLERS area – No 3 Section at BERLES area – – The whole being its front occupied by 46th DIVN. Coy. Transport with Horses, Mtd. personnel & Details remain at SOUASTRE.	
HENU	22		Nos 1, 2 & 3 Sections working on Strong Points on Divisional Line. No 4. Section at R.E. Workshops.	
	23		Same as 22nd, with the addition of Infantry Parties working (clearing C.Ts).	
	24		Same as 23rd	
	25	1 a.m.	Received orders from Adjt. to be prepared to move at short notice any time after 5 a.m. (Enemy reported fallen back on next Corps Area on our Right)	
		10 a.m.	"Stand by" order cancelled – Work as 23rd.	

R.F. Green Maj. OC 504 R by R.E.

Vol 3

Confidential

War Diary
of
504th Field Coy R.E.

from 26-2-17 to 26-3-17

Volume II

Army Form C. 2118.

WAR DIARY
or
INTELLIGENCE SUMMARY.
(Erase heading not required.)

504 Fd. Coy. R.E.

Place	Date	Hour	Summary of Events and Information	Remarks and references to Appendices
	Feb-17			
HENU	26		Work as on 23rd & preceeding days – 1 casualty (N° 2872 Pte. Pinnock of 2/5th Bn Royal Fusiliers) reported from BERLES – slightly wounded.	
	27		N°s 1, 2, & 3 Sections same work as previous day.	CRE: orders N° 4 of 26-2-17
		2.15pm	Coy H.Q. & N° 4 Section move to SOUASTRE in accordance with CRE's order.	
SOUASTRE		4 pm	Party of 1 NCO & 8 Sappers sent to FONQUEVILLERS to report to O.C. 4th Bn Leicestershire Regt. to take part – in operations – party carried Tubes of Ammonal to enemy wire to make gaps – on reaching enemy wire it was found (that) passed without use of explosives – party wire returned whilst infantry advanced into GOMMECOURT. Then returned whilst infantry advanced Communication Trench from front	
FONQUEVILLE-RS	28	9 am	N° 1 Section employed on making Communication Trench from front line trench to enemy's front line system. N° 4 Section employed cutting extra gaps in enemy's wire at GOMME-COURT.	
		3.30pm	Both the above parties under the command of 1st Lieut. Orme compelled to cease work by hostile shell fire – two casualties, N° 506385 Sapper Wheatley H.W. (seriously wounded) & N° 506586 Sapper Heath W.P. (slightly wounded).	
			N°s 2 & 3 Sections employed on work at BIENVILLERS & BERLES as on 27th.	

Army Form C. 2118.

WAR DIARY
or
INTELLIGENCE SUMMARY.
(Erase heading not required.)

504 Fd. Coy. R.E.

Instructions regarding War Diaries and Intelligence Summaries are contained in F.S. Regs., Part II. and the Staff Manual respectively. Title pages will be prepared in manuscript.

Place	Date	Hour	Summary of Events and Information	Remarks and references to Appendices
FONQUEVILLERS	March 1st	1. a.m.	In accordance with instructions received from O.C. 4th Bn. Leicestershire Regt. a party of 2 N.C.Os & men were supplied by No 1. Section to go into the front line N. & N.E. of GOMMECOURT to consolidate positions reached & to block communication trenches	
		11. a.m.	The above party returned having effected their purpose except in one case where the guide supplied by 4th Bn. Leicestershire Regt. failed to get into position.	
		12 noon	No 4 Section engaged in repairing road from FONQUEVILLERS CHURCH towards GOMMECOURT.	
		6. p.m.	Nos 1 & 4 Sections commenced to repair FIFTH AVENUE & construct double track of Trench Grids (WESSEX WALK) from the head of FIFTH AVENUE to the West edge of GOMMECOURT PARK.	
			Nos. 2 & 3 Sections working at BIENVILLERS & BERLES fell relieved at 3 p.m. by 4th Div. R.E. - 6 casualties at BERLES - all from Gas shells - Lieut. F.W. Smith - No 506334 Sergt Thicker W - No 506493, Sapper Gough. B - No 506185 Sapper Fletcher. G. - No 506507 Driver Bauch.(F.- No 5780 Pte. Randall H.A. (2/3rd Bn. Royal Fusiliers, City of London Regt) - all removed to hospital.	

1577 Wt.W10791/1773 500,000 1/15 D.D. & L. A.D.S.S./Forms/C. 2118.

Army Form C. 2118.

WAR DIARY
or
INTELLIGENCE SUMMARY.

(Erase heading not required.)

504 Fd. Coy. R.E.

Place	Date	Hour	Summary of Events and Information	Remarks and references to Appendices
SOUASTRE	1-3-17	8.pm	Nos. 2 & 3 Sections report returned all correct from BIENVILLERS & BERLES respectively.	
FONQUEVILLERS	2-3-17	7. a.m	Lieut. Orme reports WESSEX WALK completed by Nos. 1 & 4. Sections.	C.R.E. 4.0.0 No. 6 of 1-3-17.
		10.a.m	Nos. 1 & 4 Sections leave FONQUEVILLERS having completed hand over to 465th Fd. Coy. R.E. in accordance with instructions. Concentration of Coy. completed.	
SOUASTRE	3-3-17	12. noon	Coy. overhauling stores, tools & equipment - issue if necessary. Road repairs commenced on SOUASTRE - FONQUEVILLERS Road.	order of C.R.E. 46 Div.
	4-3-17		Road repairs continued - work extended to include main road through FONQUEVILLERS so far as NO MANS LAND (exclusive)	order of C.R.E. 46 Div. of 2-3-17.
	5-3-17		Work as on 4th inst.	
	6-3-17		" " " "	
		9.p.m.	Order received from C.R.E. 58 Div. to move Coy. to BAILLEULMONT on 7th inst.	O.O. No.9 of C.R.E. 58Div. dated 6-3-17.
		11 "	" " " " 4b " " " fellows - 2 Section to HUMBERCAMP	unnumbered order of C.R.E. 46 DW. dated 6-3-17.
		"	" " " " 2 " " " POMMIER	
		"	" " " " 3 " " " LARBRET	
	7-3-17	9. a.m.	Coy. moved as follows - Coy. H.Q. to LARBRET Nos. 1 & 2 Section to HUMBERCAMP " 3rd " " POMMIER	
LARBRET.		2.p.m.	Move completed. Reconnaisance made of new Strong Points on Div. Line near BELLACOURT.	

Army Form C. 2118.

WAR DIARY
or
INTELLIGENCE SUMMARY

504 Fd. Coy. R.E.

(Erase heading not required.)

Place	Date	Hour	Summary of Events and Information	Remarks and references to Appendices
LARBRET	8-3-17	9. am	Sections moved as follows – No 2. Section HUMBERCAMP to POMMIER. (to replace No 4. Section) " 4 " " POMMIER " BELLACOURT (for new work on Div. Line)	
	9-3-17		No 1. Section placed at disposal of G.O.C. 173 Inf Bde & employed on Support Line Trenches. " 2 & 3 Sections employed on S.P.s on Div. Line. Sections employed as follows – No 1 Section. Improving & Repairing Support Line Trenches. " 2 " " Work in Div. Line at BIENVILLERS " 3 " " " " " " BERLES " 4 " " " " " " BELLACOURT	
	10-3-17		Owing to less accommodation being available in POMMIER due to damage caused by hostile shell fire – Sections moved as follows – No 2. Section. POMMIER to HUMBERCAMP. " 3 " " " BERLES.	O.O. No 10 of C.R.E. 55 D.W. dated 10-3-17.
HUMBERCAMP	11-3-17		Work continued as on 9th inst. POMMIER & BERLES shelled at intervals. Reconnaissance made for siting new Machine Gun Emplacements & Fire Positions on Div. Line. Coy. H.q. moved from LARBRET to HUMBERCAMP.	
	12-3-17		Work as on 9th. Reconnaissance to site two new S.P.s in Support Line on Bde. Front. No 5034 Pte. Hatch of 2/4th Bn London Regt. (attached) wounded at BELLACOURT.	
	13-3-17		Work as on 9th. Reconnaissance made of BIENVILLERS – MONCHY Road in view of expected advance.	

Army Form C. 2118.

WAR DIARY
or
INTELLIGENCE SUMMARY.
(Erase heading not required.)

504 Fd Coy R.E.

Instructions regarding War Diaries and Intelligence Summaries are contained in F.S. Regs., Part II. and the Staff Manual respectively. Title pages will be prepared in manuscript.

Place	Date	Hour	Summary of Events and Information	Remarks and references to Appendices
POMMIER	14-3-17		Moves as follows :— Coy. H.Q. HUMBERCAMP to POMMIER	O.O. Nos. 11 & 12 of C.R.E. 56 D.V. dated March 13th & 14th respectively.
			No 1. Section " " " BIENVILLERS	
			" 2 " " " "	
			" 4 " " BELLACOURT " HUMBERCAMP.	
	15-3-17		Work on Div¹. Line or BERLES. & on Support Trenches.	
			Work on Div¹. Line at BIENVILLERS & BERLES	
			" Support " on Brigade Front. (173rd Bdy Note).	
			" Dugouts for Stragglers Posts.	
	16-3-17		Work as on 15th.	
	17-3-17		Work as on 15th.	
		6.p.m.	Telegram received from C.R.E. 56 Div. ordering work to commence on BIENVILLERS–MONCHY Road.	
		7.p.m.	Work commenced by No 1. Section	
	18-3-17	2.a.m.	Road cleared & trenches filled in as far as Enemy Front Line Trench. — 2/2nd Bn. London Regt able to pass through.	
		7.a.m.	Enemy trenches filled in & barricades cleared sufficiently to allow R.F.A. to pass through.	
		9.a.m.	No 3. Section relieves No 1. Section.	
			No 2 " Clearing HANNES CAMP – MONCHY Road.	
			Road made passable through MONCHY by 7 p.m. for everything up to light G.S. Wagons.	

Army Form C. 2118.

WAR DIARY
or
INTELLIGENCE SUMMARY.

(Erase heading not required.)

Instructions regarding War Diaries and Intelligence Summaries are contained in F. S. Regs., Part II. and the Staff Manual respectively. Title pages will be prepared in manuscript.

Place	Date	Hour	Summary of Events and Information	Remarks and references to Appendices

~~Humbery~~ POMMIER	19-3-17		Moved. No 3. Section BERLES to MONCHY.
			 " 4 " HUMBERCAMP to MONCHY.
			
			 Road repair & reconstruction on following roads – BIENVILLERS – MONCHY
			 MONCHY – ADINFER
			 MONCHY – RANSART.
			
			 Orders received to move Coy. H.Q. to BELLACOURT with advanced billets at RANSART.
			 Application made & approved by CRE. 56 Div. to move as follows :—
			      Coy. H.Q. to RANSART.
			      No 2. Section " "
			      No 1 " to ADINFER.
				O.O. No 13 of CRE. 56 Div. dated 19-3-17.

RANSART	20.3.17		Moved. Coy. H.Q. to RANSART. No 2. Section " " " 1 " to ADINFER. Work continued as on 19 :" – Road deviation at ADINFER commenced. Order received to reconstruct MONCHY – BERLES Road – reconnaissance made & unfavourable report sent in.	O.O. No 14 of CRE. 56 Div. of 19-3-17 O.O. No 15 of CRE. 56 Div. of 20-3-17.
	21-3-17		Work as on 20 F. 	
		11.50 pm	Orders received to move. H.Q. & 1 Section to POMMIER & 1 Section from ADINFER to MONCHY	G.O. No 15 of 56 Div. of 21-3-17.

Army Form C. 2118.

WAR DIARY
or
INTELLIGENCE SUMMARY
(Erase heading not required.)

504 Fd. Coy. R.E.

Place	Date	Hour	Summary of Events and Information	Remarks and references to Appendices
POMMIER	22-3-17		Move. Coy. H.Q. RANSART to POMMIER. No. 2. Sectn. " " 1 " ADINFER " MONCHY. Work. Road reconstruction BIENVILLERS - MONCHY - MONCHY - ADINFER. Road deviation at ADINFER completed (less road metal not obtainable) and put to take 3 ton lorries.	
	23-3-17		Work " on 22nd + Road repair at POMMIER	
	24-3-17		Work " on 23rd. all roads in Coy. area fit to take 3 ton lorries. Lieut. B.O. Brunting & Lieut. F.W. Burnett reported for duty from England.	
	25-3-17		Work " on 23rd	
	26-3-17		Work on 2-3rd	

Army Form C. 2118.

Vol 4
504 Fd. Coy. R.E.

WAR DIARY
or
INTELLIGENCE SUMMARY.
(Erase heading not required.)

Place	Date	Hour	Summary of Events and Information	Remarks and references to Appendices
POMMIER	27-3-17		Coy. distributed as follows :– H.Q. & No. 2. Section – POMMIER Nos. 1, 3 & 4 Section – MONCHY-AU-BOIS.	
	28-3-17	9. a.m.	Road clearing – repairing & reconstruction at POMMIER – MONCHY-AU-BOIS and ADINFER.	
		2. p.m.	Same as 27th.	
			Move. Nos. 3 & 4 Section to POMMIER.	
	29-3-17		Move. H.Q. & Nos. 2, 3 & 4 Section POMMIER to LUCHEUX.	
LUCHEUX	30-3-17		Move No. 1. Section MONCHY-AU-BOIS to LUCHEUX.	
	31-3-17		Company repairing camp site.	
BOQUEMAISON	1-4-17		Move. LUCHEUX to BOQUEMAISON.	
LANEUVILLE	2-4-17		Move BOQUEMAISON to LANEUVILLE.	
BOQUEMAISON	4-4-17		Move LANEUVILLE to BOQUEMAISON. 2 Lieut. W. H. Shaddock reported for duty from England.	
		4. p.m.	Orders received by telegram as follows from General Staff, VII Corps – Coy. (less 1 officer & 10 other ranks) to move on 5-4-17 into MONCHY area – Sappers to be conveyed by Motor Bus – Transport to move on 5th to WARLINCOURT and on 6th to MONCHY. 1 officer & 10 other ranks to report to Field. Jenkins R.E. at Town Majors Office, ARRAS.	

Army Form C. 2118.

WAR DIARY
or
INTELLIGENCE SUMMARY.
(Erase heading not required.)

504 Fd Coy R.E.

Place	Date	Hour	Summary of Events and Information	Remarks and references to Appendices
BOQUEMAISON	5-4-17		Move as follows:- Three Officers & 120 other ranks by motorlorry to MOTCHY-AU-BOIS. Seven Officers & 300 " " " " " route march to WARLINCOURT. 1 Officer (Lieut Row) & 10 otherranks by motor lorry to ARRAS for demolition work.	
MONCHY AU BOIS	6-4-17	6 p.m.	Reported for orders to C.R.E. 21st Divn. at ADINFER WOOD - received orders to work under & be attached to 21st Divn. Seven officers & 300 other ranks WARLINCOURT to MONCHY AU BOIS. Two Officers & No.1. Section MONCHY AU BOIS to ADINFER.	
	7-4-17		Work. No.1. Section - Hutting at ADINFER WOOD. MONCHY - DOUCHY LES AYETTE Nos 2-3&4 " - Preparing Dry weather Vehicle Tracks - MONCHY - ADINFER. Reconnaissances made for Vehicle Tracks - RANSART - MONCHY ADINFER - BOIRY St RICTRUDE.	
	8-4-17		Work Same as 7th.	
	9-4-17		Work Same as 7th. with the addition of assistance given to 97th Fd Coy R.E. at BOIRY St RICTRUDE.	
	10-4-17		Same as 9th.	
	11-4-17		Same as 9th.	

Army Form C. 2118.

WAR DIARY
or
INTELLIGENCE SUMMARY.
(Erase heading not required.)

504 Fd Cy R.E.

Place	Date	Hour	Summary of Events and Information	Remarks and references to Appendices
MONCHY AU BOIS	11-4-17	5 p.m.	Following telegram received -* To 504th Field Cy R.E. S.P.72 of 11-4-17. Following message received from C in C. is to be circulated to all ranks aaa begins aaa My warmest congratulations on the important success achieved by you yesterday aaa The manner in which the operations were prepared and carried out reflects the highest credit on Commanders Staff and Troops aaa Please convey to all who were employed my appreciation of the great skill and gallantry shewn by them aaa end. - From C.R.E. 21st D.W.	*Original Telegram attached to this sheet
	12-4-17		Work as on 9th	
		6 p.m.	Orders received for move to BUS LES ARTOIS.	
BUS-LES-ARTOIS	13-4-17	3 p.m.	Move from MONCHY AU BOIS to BUS LES ARTOIS completed.	
	14-4-17		Company cleaning stores - vehicles etc. Advanced Party sent with units of 173 Inf. Bde. to ACHIET-LE-GRAND.	
ACHIET LE GRAND	15-4-17		Move from BUS-LES-ARTOIS to ACHIET-LE-GRAND.	
	16-4-17		Company employed on R.E. Service for 173 Inf Bde.	
	17-4-17		Same on 16th with the addition of erecting Divl. Hq. Camp at BIHUCOURT.	

"A" Form.
MESSAGES AND SIGNALS.

Prefix ...... Code ...... m.	Words / Charge	This message is on a/c of:	Recd. at .... m.
Office of Origin and Service Instructions.	Sent At .... m. To By	............Service. (Signature of "Franking Officer.")	Date .... From .... By ....

TO — 504th (Field) CoRE

Sender's Number.	Day of Month.	In reply to Number.	AAA.
S.P. 72	11		

Following message received from C in C:- "I watched from beginning to end the operation carried out yesterday and the manner in which it was planned and carried out reflects the highest credit on everyone. All ranks who were employed took part in the great skill and gallantry shown by them and all. Please convey to all ranks my warmest congratulations on the success achieved by them yesterday and the manner in which the operations were prepared and carried out reflects the highest credit on all. Please convey to all ranks my appreciation of the great skill and gallantry shown by them."

From: C.R.E.
Place: 21st Div
Time:

Army Form C. 2118.

WAR DIARY
or
INTELLIGENCE SUMMARY.

(Erase heading not required.)

504 Fd Cy R/E.

Place	Date	Hour	Summary of Events and Information	Remarks and references to Appendices
ACHIET LE GRAND	18-4-17		Same as 17^{15}	
	19-4-17		"	
	20-4-17		"	
	21-4-17		"	
	22-4-17		Commenced 8 Days scheme of Training in addition to campaign Eng Service for 173 Bde & Divl. H.Q.	
	23-4-17		Same as 22nd	
	24-4-17		" " 22nd — Eng. Services for Divl. H.Q. completed.	
	25-4-17		Same as 22nd — All Eng. Services discontinued.	
	26-4-17		Training Scheme.	

R.J.Wrees-Athur
O.C. 504 Fd Cy R.E.

Instructions regarding War Diaries and Intelligence Summaries are contained in F. S. Regs., Part II. and the Staff Manual respectively. Title pages will be prepared in manuscript.

1577 Wt. W10791/1773 500,000 1/15 D. D. & L. A.D.S.S./Forms/C. 2118.

Army Form C. 2118.

58/

504 Fd Coy R.E

WAR DIARY
or
INTELLIGENCE SUMMARY.
(Erase heading not required.)

Place	Date	Hour	Summary of Events and Information	Remarks and references to Appendices
ACHIET-LE GRAND	27-4-17		Training Scheme	Vol 5
	30-4-17			R.A.
	1-5-17	11 am	Inspection by C.R.E. 58 D.V.	R.A.
	2-5-17		Experiments with Bangalore Torpedoes & Greene Training.	R.A.
VAULX VRAUCOURT	3-5-17	2 pm	Move to VAULX VRAUCOURT.	R.A.
	4-5-17		Taking over works from 511th Fd. Coy. R.E.	R.A.
	5-5-17		No 1. Section - making ramps to Horse Troughs at MORY. Remainder of Coy - Road repairing on MORY - ECOUST Road	R.A.
	6-5-17		Whole Coy - Road repairing & superving construction of shelters for R.F.A.	R.A.
	7-5-17	1 pm	Maj Ancrum proceeded on leave to England. Capt Tanby in charge of Coy. Lt V.G. PEARCE reported for duty. Whole Company - Road repairing Supervising construction of shelters for R.F.A.	R.A. W.H.T.

Army Form C. 2118.

504 Fd Coy R.E.

WAR DIARY
INTELLIGENCE SUMMARY.
(Erase heading not required.)

Place	Date	Hour	Summary of Events and Information	Remarks and references to Appendices
VAULX VRAUCOURT	8-5-17	—	Whole Company Road-repairing. Supervision of shelters for R.T.O.	W.H.T.
	9-5-17	7.30 p.m.	Company, less Transport, moved to S.5.c.5.5. (Map Ref. 57.C.N.W. 1/20.000). Capt. Tamlyn reported to G.O.C. 175th Brigade. Capt. Tamlyn. 11 Lt. Row. Lt. Burnett & 11 Lt. Orme made reconnaissance of 175th Brigade Front for siting of strong points mine.	W.H.T.
LAGNICOURT	10-5-17	10.a.m.	Lt. Burnett made reconnaissance of noon C.28.d.10-6 to C.23.d.10-4 supervising. 11 Lt. Row Sap. making strong points. 11 Lt. Burnett, Orme, Tamlyn were in 175th Brigade from by Infantry working parties.	W.H.T.
		8.p.m	Sappers Stokes, Guinn & Rutcher still wounded. 11 Lt. Orme with four sections and Infantry working parties.	
	11-5-17	8.p.m	11 Lt. Burnett & 175th Brigade. wiring front at ACHIET LE GRAND to G.O.C. 173rd Infantry Brigade. Capt. Tamlyn reported to B.30.a.6.7.	W.H.T.
VAULX VRAUCOURT	12-5-17	6.p.m	Company returned to B.30.a.6.7. Capt. Tamlyn reported to O/C 15th Australian Field Co. R.E. to ascertain from uncompleted constructing wire entanglements.	W.H.T.
	13-5-17	a.m 11.0	Capt. Tamlyn reported to G.O.C. 173rd Infantry Brigade took instructions as to constructing entanglements. 11 Lt. Row & 11 Lt. Burnett with 2 sections	
		8.p.m	constructing wire entanglements.	W.H.T.

Army Form C. 2118.

504 Fd Coy R.E.

WAR DIARY
or
INTELLIGENCE SUMMARY.
(Erase heading not required.)

Place	Date	Hour	Summary of Events and Information	Remarks and references to Appendices
VAULX - VRACOURT.	14.5.17	10.0 a.m.	Capt Tamlyn reporting to 2.6.6. 173rd Brigade & receiving instructions to construct shelters at B.9.d.8.4. Lieut-Cruse & ii Hendersh with 2 Sections excavating bank spilling roundtop.	
		9.pm	ii Lt Rows & 1 Section building shelters. ii Lt Burnett, attempted reconnaissance of trench & road U.28.c.7.3 — U.28.d.2.9 Casualties Corpl Rewney & Sapper Hulbert. Shell wounds.	W.T.
	15.5.17	8 am	Lt Bunting & 1 Section continuing erection of Brigade headquarter shelters.	
		7.pm	ii Lt Burnett making reconnaissance of trench & road U.28.c.7.3 — U.28.d.2.9	W.T.
	16.5.17	1.pm	ii Lt Crisse & 1 Section improving entrances to Brigade Headquarters shelters.	
		2 pm	Capt Tamlyn with C.R.E. attempted reconnaissance of Ecoust - Bullecourt road.	W.T.
	17.5.17	8 am	Lt Bunting & 1 Section. Erection of Shelter for Battalion Headquarters at B.9.d.8.4.	W.T.
		11 am	ii Lt Rows & 1 Section, deepening & improving trenches at B.16.c.4.3	

Army Form C. 2118.

WAR DIARY
or
INTELLIGENCE SUMMARY.
(Erase heading not required.)

504 Fd Coy R.E.

Place	Date	Hour	Summary of Events and Information	Remarks and references to Appendices
VAULX - VRAUCOURT.	18.5.17	8.0 am	Lt-Reeve with Infantry party repairing Mory-Ecoust road.	W.A.T.
			Lt-Bennett 1 section reworking Strong Point. 57.C.N.W. B.17.6.7.1.	
		10.30 pm	Lt-Bunting 110 sappers. Tracing Communication Trench 57.51.D.S.W. U.28.d.6.9 * Congratulatory Messages from 1st Division's Commander 5th Army. to 58th Division(2) attached G.O.C. 55 Div. 1st to 173 Inf Bde 17 Bn 1st Bn to 173 Inf Bde	
MORY	19.5.17	8.0 am	Lieut Shadwell & 3 Sappers. erecting Bangalore Beats at 57.C.N.M. B.21.6.8.0.	W.A.T.
BIHUCOURT			Lieut-Grew Hutton. Constructing Grenade Trocks.	
MORY		"	Bennett. Hutton. Excavating Strong Point. 57.G.N.W. B.17.6.7.1	
VAULX - VRAUCOURT.		"	Reeve. with Infantry party repairing Mory - Ecourt road.	
		"	Row. Hickman constructing improving second line defences. 57.C.N.M. B.18.C.7.1.	
			Major Lockett returned to duty.	R.F.1.
	20.5.17		Work Same as 19th	
	21.5.17		" " "	R.F.1.
	22.5.17		" " " wire addition & Improving O.P.s for R.F.A. at 57.C.N.W. B.6.1.6.2.	R.F.1.
	23.5.17		Work same as 22nd. with addition of night wiring in front of ECOUST.	R.F.1 attached
			Congratulation message received from G.O.C. 58 Div. to 173 Inf Bde.	
	24.5.17		Capt. Tulloch left on 10 days leave, night wiring at 57.C.N.W.C.3.2.1.0 C.2.6.7.8	R.F.1.
	25.5.17		Work as 24.5.17 - Wire addition - Wire work at ECOUST - Laying C.T. & making new C.T.s at Heads. (3).	R.F.1

O/C 503rd Field Coy RE
O/C 504th Field Coy RE
O/C 511th Field Coy RE

Following message from DHQ is repeated for information. Begins Group 17th aaa Fifth Corps wire dated 16th inst begins aaa Fifth Army wire begins aaa Please convey to the 58th Division the Army Commander's thanks for the resolute defence of the line during the night of the 14/15th aaa It is evident from your reports that they were subjected to a series of very severe attacks and that their conduct throughout was most creditable aaa ends

E. M. Newell
Lieut. Colonel. R.E (T)
C.R.E. 58th (London) Division

S838
18.5.17

Brig. General Freyberg, V.C., D.S.O.
Commanding, 173rd Infantry Brigade.

      I should like to express to all ranks of the 173rd Infantry Brigade, my gratitude and admiration for the determination, and fine fighting spirit, with which, you held your ground under very heavy shell fire, and repulsed the strong German attacks, between 12th and 14th of May. By your actions you have brought us great credit, and have given us further reason to be proud of the 58th (London) Division, to which we belong.

                         (Signed) H.D. FANSHAWE, Maj.General,
                                  Comdg., 58th Division.

23-5-17.

173rd Infantry Brigade

The following messages are published for information:-

To:- 173rd Infantry Brigade. 13/5/17.
"Fifth Army wire dated 12th aaa following received from Commander-in-Chief begins aaa I congratulate all your troops on the complete successes of the various attacks made yesterday and this morning aaa These successes are very satisfactory not only in themselves but as showing that the enemy is beginning to weaken under the repeated heavy blows inflicted on him during all the hard fighting of the past five weeks aaa ends aaa Addressed all concerned aaa
                58th Division"

To:- 173rd Infantry Brigade. 17/5/17.
"Fifth Corps wire dated 16th inst. begins aaa Fifth Army wire begins aaa Please convey to the 58th Division the Army Commanders thanks for the resolute defence of the line during the night of the 14/15th aaa It is evident from your reports that they were subjected to a series of very severe attacks and that their conduct throughout was most creditable aaa ends aaa addressed 173rd Inf. Bde.
                58th Division".

To:- 173rd Infantry Brigade. 17/5/17.
"Following from 7th Division begins aaa All Ranks of the 7th Division offer their heartiest congratulations to you and your Division on your success in the final capture of BULLECOURT to-day aaa None knew better than ourselves the difficult task the 58th Divn. had to undertake and we are full of admiration for gallantry and dash with which it was accomplished.
                58th Division".

To:- 173rd Infantry Brigade. 18/5/17.
"Very many thanks for message greatly appreciated by all ranks under my command aaa Troops were greatly stimulated by the fine example of your stubborn defence on previous days.
                174th Infantry Brigade"

                              Headquarters,
                              14th Aust. Inf.Bde.

"I am sending you this line to say how much we appreciated the very willing and prompt way in which Lt.Col.Beresford sent up a detachment to hold part of our front line whilst the 54th Battalion counter-attacked.
    Major Lecky took the step of asking for this assistance as his Companies had been so decimated by the bombardment and it required all he had left to regain the portion of trench occupied by the Germans.
    Will you kindly convey my sincere thanks to Lt.-Col.Beresford for his prompt action and for the valuable assistance of the detachment of the 2/3rd London Regiment.
                Yours Sincerely,
                (Sd) C.G.HOBKIRK, Br.-Gen.
17/5/17.   Comdg., 14th Aust.Infantry Brigade."

Army Form C. 2118.

WAR DIARY
or
INTELLIGENCE SUMMARY.

(Erase heading not required.)

504 Fd Coy R.E.

Place	Date	Hour	Summary of Events and Information	Remarks and references to Appendices
VAUX - VRAUCOURT	26-5-17.		W of C. Same as 25th with addition of work on "Yellow Line" - (sitting - trenching & spitlocking).	R.S.

R Thorowthnj.
O.C. 504 Fd Cy R.E.

Army Form C. 2118.

504 Fd Coy R.E.

WAR DIARY
or
INTELLIGENCE SUMMARY.
(Erase heading not required.)

Instructions regarding War Diaries and Intelligence Summaries are contained in F. S. Regs., Part II. and the Staff Manual respectively. Title pages will be prepared in manuscript.

Place	Date	Hour	Summary of Events and Information	Remarks and references to Appendices
VAULX -VRAUCOURT	2/5/17		Work same as 24th	R.E.
	26.5.17		" " "	R.E.
	29.5.17		" " "	R.E.
	30.5.17		Orders received that from 30th May Coy. would be at the disposal of C.O.C. 173 Inf Bde for R.E. work.	R.A.
			In accordance with orders received previous day sections detailed as follows — No 1. Section 1st Lieut Orme & 2/Lieut Burnett attached to 2/4th Bn Royal Irish Rifles	
			" 2 " " " Burnett	" 2/3rd "
			" 3 " " Lieut Pearce	" 2/2nd "
			" 4 " " 2/Lieut Row	" 2/4 R "
	8 pm		Lieut Pearce & 2/Lieut Orme with their parties proceeded to 2/1st & 2/2nd Bns Royal Irish in trenches W. of BULLECOURT. Work on O.P.s to R.F.A.	R.A.
	31.5.17		Lieut Pearce & 2/Lieut Orme make reconnaissance of front line Row proceed with their parties to 2/3rd Bn R.F.R. & Burnett " " " " 2/4th Bn R.F. at MORY COPSE respectively ST. LEGER and 2/4th Bn R.F. at Storey Point, by 1st & 3rd Sections. Construction of O.P.s & Dug Out for R.F.A.	

504 2nd Cav R.E.
Vol 6

On His Majesty's Service.

To O/C No 14 Offrs C
O/C Offrs Cyprus

[signature]

Army Form C. 2118.

WAR DIARY
or
INTELLIGENCE SUMMARY.
(Erase heading not required.)

504 Fd Coy R/E

Place	Date	Hour	Summary of Events and Information	Remarks and references to Appendices
VAULX - VRAUCOURT	1-6-17		1st Lieut. Orme & No 1. Section - Wiring outposts Lieut. Pearce & No 3 " - Trench Improvement } Supervision. " " " - Wiring Strong Point " Burnett & No 2 " - O.T. Construction between outposts " " " No 4 " - Wiring Instruction to 2/3rd Bn. R.F. " " " " 2/4 " " " Rowe & No 4 " - " " " 2/4 " " Dug out & O.P. construction for R.F.A.	
	6.pm		Move of Coy. H.Q. completed to MORY COPSE E. (Ref. Sheet 57 C.N.W. B.15.c.9.f) R.F.1. O.31.	
MORY COPSE	2-6-17		Work as same as 1-6-17	
	3-6-17		Work - Was Dug out & O.P. Construction for R.F.A. Reliefs 1st Lieut Burnett & No 2 Section relieved 1st Lieut. Orme & No 1 Section R.F. " " " " in No 4 " Lieut Pearce & No 3 " R.F. on N.E. &	
	5.30pm		Camp shelled with 38 centimetre gun - Shells falling on S.E. sides of camp - no casualties.	
	4-6-17		Work - Dug out & O.P. Construction for R.F.A. No 4 Section - Dug Out Construction in No 1. Subsector Bripile Line Camp of Coy H.Q. & detail moved to ERVILLERS (Ref Sheet. 57c.N.W 1st Lieut. Orme - Sick to Hospital.	B.14.a.4.8) R.F.1.

WAR DIARY
or
INTELLIGENCE SUMMARY

Army Form C. 2118.

504 Fd Coy R.E.

Place	Date	Hour	Summary of Events and Information	Remarks and references to Appendices
ERVILLERS	5.6.17		No 1. Section. Overhauling Kits & general cleaning up.	
			" 2 " Improving quarters in 1st line with 2/5th Bn Lond Regt.	
			" 3 " Overhauling Kits & general cleaning up.	
			" 4 " Dug Out construction.	
			Special Party. Dug out & O.P. construction for R.A.	R.W.A.
		10.pm	O.C. Coy. made special reconnaissance in No Mans Land for Brig. Gen. Cmdg 173 Inf. Bde — Assembly line successfully marked out & taped its plan	R.W.A
			Capt Tomlinson returned from leave.	
	6.6.17		No 1. Section. R.E. Services at ST LEGER.	
			2 " " Same.	
			3 " " Rebuilding shelters at MORY.	
			4 " " Dug Out construction in line.	
			Special Party O.P. & Dug out construction for R.A.	R.W.A
			Lieut Sheddick Party. Construction shelters for H.Q. 173 Inft Bde.	
			Casualty. No 506593. L Cpl Cole R.J. Wounded - to hospital.	
	7.6.17		Work as on 6th.	
		11 pm	Lieut Brunwin & party of No 2 Section came out of the line & reported to Coy. H.Q. — H.Q./3rd Bn Lond Regt. Being relieved by 2/7th Bn Lond Regt.	R.W.A

Army Form C. 2118.

WAR DIARY
or
INTELLIGENCE=SUMMARY.

(Erase heading not required.)

50 4 Fd. Coy. R.E.

Instructions regarding War Diaries and Intelligence Summaries are contained in F. S. Regs., Part II. and the Staff Manual respectively. Title pages will be prepared in manuscript.

Place	Date	Hour	Summary of Events and Information	Remarks and references to Appendices
ERVILLERS	8.6.17		Work as on 6th. Lieut. Burnett party returning Knuckle Clean up.	
	9.6.17	11.30 p.m.	Raid carried out in conjunction with Party from 2/1st Bn. London Regt. on the KNUCKLE TRENCH, N.W. of BULLECOURT for the purpose of destroying M.G. Emplacements in addition to the usual objects. Raid was entirely successful – one concrete building being stocked with Gun extra charges & a full description of other being obtained. ✱ Casualties – 2 slightly wounded – remained on duty. Party consisted of N° 506392 2/Cpl. Baker. C. " 506480 L/Cpl. Gillham. J. " 506460 Sap. Barnes, F. " 506457 " Cook. C.H. " 506663 " Drewett. E. " 506760 " Hack. W.E. " 506416 " Phelps. F. " 506521 " Coward. C. " 506423 " Stenson. F. " 486150 " Devine. C. " 506213 " Eames A.W. " 506068 " Redman E.Y.	✱ Intelligence Summary required on 9-6-17 attached.

R.J.L.

173rd. INFANTRY BRIGADE.

Intelligence Summary of Raid on the Knuckle between
U.20.b.9.5. to U.20.a.6.8.

At 11.30.p.m. on the 8/6/17 a party of the 2/1st. Battalion London Regt under the command of Major.G.Thompson.M.C. consisting of ii.Lieut.Selden and ii.Lieut.Ward with 10.N.C.O's and 48.Men of the 2/1st.London Regt and 504th.Field Coy.R.E. entered the enemy trenches at the KNUCKLE.
The following information was obtained :-

    A. From our own party.
    B. From a N.C.O. of the 99th.R.I.R. captured and examined at Brigade Headquarters by an Intelligence Officer of the V.Corps.

A. 1. There was no Rifle, or Machine Gun or unusual activity on the part of the enemy before ZERO. The raiding party assembled unobserved by the enemy.
2. Our artillery Barrage was opened promptly and simultaneously at 11.30.p.m. and was powerful and effective.
3. Ordinary Very Light activity only before ZERO. Green twin star signals fired by enemy on the opening of our barrage. During the raid many green twin, a few reds, and a number of orange lights bursting into several stars, were fired. On the cessation of our barrage at 12.20. several Golden Rain were fired.
4. All parties report that enemy wire forms no obstacle.
5. The condition of enemy's trenches varies, but is generally fair. Theye are about 12.Feet wide from paraper to parados and very deep with a greater batter than usual.
6. Enemy resistance varied. There was little opposition to the entry of our men beyond a few bombs and slight rifle fire from support line which quickly ceased. On the right the blocking party met with some resistance and some bayonet fighting ensued before the enemy bolted over the top to his support line. No enemy shell fire was put down for 8.minutes when he seemed uncertain of locality of raid, shelling half-way across no-mans land, and more heavily to the flanks than on the fron attacked. Later he shelled his own front line and wire at the KNUCKLE with a moderately heavy barrage.
7. MEBUS
(a) At U.20.b.15.52. was intact and party detailed to destry it were engaged in fighting with some of the enemy. This MEBUS is reported as having a dug-out shaft in rear with steps leading down.
(b) MEBUS at U.20.a.85.65. was occupied and the prisoner captured came out of it. The remainder of the occupants after crying "Kamerad" failed to come out. As more prisoners were required, ii.Lieut.Selden went inside to get them. A bomb was thrown however and the occupants were accordingly killed.
(c) MEBUS at U.20.a.80.80. was occupied by the enemy and bombed with a "P" Bomb by ii.Lieut.Ward, killing the occupants and the R.E.successfully destroyed it, blowing the roof off.
8. The existence of a dug-out in C.T. is confirmed, but the entrance in C.T. is blown in and destroyed by shell fire. The existence of one of the dug-out shafts in rear of the front line is confirmed. It is at the bottom of a very large crater like hole at about U.20.a.90.65, and runs down apparently to a great depth with steps leading down. It was bombed but not entered as it was not found until after our barrage was back on the front line by Corporal Thornhill, who had got seperated from his group and returned after the raiding party was back in our lines.

9. There was no evidence of M.G. emplacements in front of wire or trench.
10. No gas grenades were thrown but stick grenades were used, and occassional rifle shots fired. One M.G. to the left of our party fired about 11.40.pm and from 11.55.p.m. M.G's were active to the S. of the KNUCKLE.
11. No ration or store dumps were seen but there was a rack of rifles in the Mebus at U.20.85.65.
12. No machine gun emplacements were seen. There is slit loop-hole about 5" high and about 3.feet long running horizontally across right semi-circular front of the Mebus at U.20.a.80.80. closed by a steel shutter. Traversing fire would be possible from it, or it may be an O.P. slit.
13. An accurate estimate of enemy casualties is impossible but about 20.were killed in the trenches by the raiders and the barrage fire was observed to catch several who escaped from the trenches towards the support line, over the top. Several men report seeing enemy advancing from the support line over the top and caught by our barrage.

B. Prisoner is a N.C.O. of the 99th.R.I.R. and was communicative and apparently reliable. He states that :-
1. The enemy did not expect an attack until our barrage opened.
2. The wire between front line and support forms no obstacle.
3. He was unaware that we did not intend to occupy the trenches entered and was confident an immediate counter-attack would be launched by the troops in the support line which is full of dug-outs. Orders to this effect are definite.
4. The battalion strength is four companies. The company strength is 120, each of three companies holds a 400.Yard front. Three companies have one platoon in the front line, and two in the support and the whole of the fourth is in support line. The reserve battalion is in copse and "Hoop" trenches, and the rest billets are at RUMANCOURT.
Reliefs are effected from the ARRAS-CAMBRAI road without going through any village. Each company front has four Mebus which prisoner maintains firmly are merely concrete shelters for trench garrison of 1.N.C.O & 8.Men, and that no other troops hold the front line.
5. Hot meals have been regularly provided for front line troops every night, and rations are good.
6. He is emphatic that there are no machine guns in the front line and that the 99th.R.I.R. have not yet been supplied with their light machine guns. The 190th Regiment on their left have their light machine guns and also the 55th.Regiment on their right. The right regimental boundary is the factory road, and there is a strong post at the HUMP cross roads.
Only one MEBUS, however, is in the front line of the 55th.Regt.
7. He is certain there is no tunnel communication between front line and support.
8. He maintains there are no dug-outs other than the Mebus in the front line.
9. Each Company sends out a patrol of 1.N.C.O. and 8.Men nightly to observe for working parties and endeavour to cut off our patrols.
10. During the past few days, heavy shelling has caused a number of casualties.
11. Prisoner states that light signals to Artillery are changed daily and are in force until 6.0.a.m. and that he thinks the S.O.S. last night was Red.
12. The prisoner is an Alsatian from STRASBOURG.

      (Sd) C.J.GRAHAM. ii.Lieut.
       I.O. 173rd.Infantry Brigade.
9/6/17.   for.Brigade Major.

Army Form C. 2118.

WAR DIARY
or
INTELLIGENCE SUMMARY.
(Erase heading not required.)

504 Fd. Coy. R.E.

Place	Date	Hour	Summary of Events and Information	Remarks and references to Appendices
ERVILLERS	9-6-17		No 1 Section - R.E. Services ST LEGER. " 2 " - Dippin C.T. in River Bed from PELICAN AVENUE - approx. length 250' " 3 " - Improvin quarters at MORY. " 4 " - Dugout construction & Trench excavation in line. Instructional path - Shelter & Prisoner Detention Enclosure construction for H.Q. 175 Inf Bde.	
			Special Party - Shelter construction R.A. Operation Orders No 25 received from Bde Maj. 175 Inf Bde * Works on 9th - Lieut Sheddock's party. Operation Order No 203 received from C.R.E. 58 Div ⊕ Special Parties preparing for Scheme. Capt Williamson commences construction in steel works attached to 175 Inf Bde.	*attached ⊕attached
	10-6-17	4 pm	Order received postponing Scheme of Operation # WORK - No 2 Section, cutting steps in LONE TRENCH. No 4 Section & Detail - Dug out & shelter construction in line for 2/4 Bn Lond Regt & H.Q. 175 Inf Bde Special Party - Shelter construction for R.A.	#attached
	11-6-17	8pm	Special Parties which had concentrated in ST LEGER for Scheme moved to Billets - No 1 & 2 Section to Coy H.Q. " 3 " to MORY Quarters.	

SECRET   Copy.No:-12.

173rd. INFANTRY BRIGADE.

Operation Order No:-25.   8th June 1917.

Reference attached Maps :- BULLECOURT 1/10.000.
CHERISY. 1/10.000   - 10.per Battalion.
and Operation
Map   A. Assembly Areas and
          Objectives, 1/5,000   - 300 to each Battalion.
       B. Hump Position, 1/2,500 - 250 to 2/2nd.London Regt.
       C. Knuckle Position
          1/1,250   - A few to 2/rd & 2/1st.Bns.
Report Map. 1. General Map.   - 100 to each Battalion.
            2. Pigeon Map.   - 25 to each Battalion.

---

1. PLAN. The 173rd. Infantry Brigade is to carry out an attack on the HINDENBURG Front Line.
   The attack will be made by moonlight, Z day and ZERO hour will be issued later.
   Troops on our right and left will co-operate with rifle, Machine Gun and Lewis Gun fire, and will undertake minor operations as outlined in para. 7.
   The objects of this attack are -
   (a) To gain ground, to kill and harass the enemy.
   (b) To improve our tactical position.
   (c) To take prisoners.

2. OBJECTIVES.
   1st.Objective. HINDENBURG Front line from U.20.b.40.17 to U.14.a.05.05.
   2nd.Objective. A line in, or commanding the Sunken Road from U.20.b.5.2. to U.14.a.05.05.. (This will not be a continuous line, but a continuous chain of Battle Patrols with Lewis Guns to act as a covering party to the main line of resistance, and to deny the sunken road to the enemy.)

3. ASSEMBLY AREAS. Units will move to their Assembly Areas by dark, and will be in their alloted positions (See Map A.) by - 30.minutes.
   The greatest care should be taken to avoid unnecessary movement and noise forward of the Railway Embankment.
   All movement into Assembly Areas, will be across the open.
   To avoid confusion guide tapes will be laid from Railway Embankment by Battalions concerned.
   All units alloted to either of the assembly areas will come under the command of O.C's.Battalions concerned from 9.p.m. on Y.Day.

4. ADVANCED BRIGADE HEADQUARTERS. Will be established in the Sunken Road at T.30.c.3.9. by 5.p.m. on Z.day.
   There will be a Brigade Report centre at U.10.b.9.2. This report centre will be used as Battalion Headquarters for centre assaulting battalion.
   There will be runner posts at
   (a) U.25.a.75.50.
   (b) T.24.d.8.2.

5. TIME TABLE OF ATTACK. The attack will be carried out in accordance with attached table of barrages. It must be clearly understood, however, that the times published are merely as a guide to the infantry, and are not orders for the exact times of assaults. It is of vital importance that the infantry should keep close up to the artillery barrage, and advance whenever it lifts

2.

6. ARTILLERY SUPPORT.	The 173rd. Infantry Brigade will be supported by the Artillery of three Divisions - the 7th, 58th, and 62nd Divisions; assisted by the Vth Corps Heavy Artillery.
7. SCHEME OF ATTACK.	The Brigade will attack with the 2/rd. Battalion on the Right, 2/1st. Battalion in the centre, and the 2/2nd. Battalion on the left. The 2/3rd, & 2/1st. Bns will attack on a four Company front. The 2/2nd. Bn will be on a three company front, with the fourth company acting as a special detachment, with a task which will be dealt with in para.8. The 1st. wave of each company will consist of two platoons in single rank. One platoon per company, less Lewis Gun section, will follow the 1st. wave at 10 paces distance to act as moppers. The 2nd. Wave of each company will be 30. paces behind the 1st. wave, and will consist of one platoon and the Lewis Gun section detached from the moppers. The advance and assault. The whole assaulting force will move forward at ZERO and get close up to the barrage.. Care should be taken to maintain the distances laid down. When the barrage lifts the 1st. wave will advance and assault the first objective and clean it up. The moppers up will be dropped to deal with any of the enemy who are in advance of their own front line - this should be done very thoroughly The 2nd. Wave will advance close to the barrage and assault the 2nd. Objective, establishing themselves as a line of battle patrols. A Company, 2/4th. Bn will take over front line from our present left to U.13.b.6.3. on Y Night from 110th Infantry Brigade under orders to be issued later. 2/4th. Bn will join up by bombing if necessary - with left of 2/2nd. Bn as soon as 1st. objective has been reached. The 2/7th. Bn on our Right, will also seize and occupy the line of the Sunken Road from U.21.c.2.3. to right of 2/rd. Bn as soon as 1st. Objective has been captured.
8. SPECIAL DETACHMENT.	The company of the 2/2nd. Bn referred to in para 7. will advance and capture enemy strong point at U.14.a.15.00 and the cross roads at U.14.c.35.85.
9. VICKERS MAXIM GUNS	The advance will be supported by the guns of the 206th., 198th, and 214th. Machine Gun Coys., and the guns of the 21st. Division. After the capture of the 2nd. Objective, O.C.206th. M.G.Co. will arrange for 8 M.Gs. to take up their position in captured German Line. O.C.206.M.G.Co. will confer with Battalion Commanders of the 2/rd. 2/1st and 2/2nd. Bns on the placing of these guns.
10. LIGHT TRENCH MORTARS.	The O.C.173rd. L.T.M. Battery will arrange for four guns to move into enemy front line as soon as the 2nd. objective is captured, and the hostile barrage has ceased. O.C.173rd. L.T.M. Battery will confer with O.C's of the 2/3rd. 2/1st and 2/2nd Bn to arrange emplacements.

11. R.E. The O.C. 504th.Field Coy.R.E. will arrange with
O's C.2/3rd, 2/1st, and 2/2nd.Bns to lend R.E. personnel.
  (a) With mobile charges of guncotton to
demolish any tunnels that may exist in the captured trenches.
  (b) For supervision in constructing strong points at:-

    U.14.c.36.95   in   2/2nd.Bn sub-sector.
    U.20.a.95.85   in   2/1st.Bn sub-sector.
    U.20.b.15.52.   in   2/3rd.Bn sub-sector.
    U.20.b. 4. 2.   in   2/3rd.Bn sub-sector.

12. ADVANCE OF BATTALION HEADQUARTERS. Battalion Headquarters will not advance until the Objective has been captured. Representatives of Headquarters will follow last wave and select a place for Headquarters and send back to notify the Bn Commander. Bn. Commanders will immediately send back location of his new H.Q. to Brigade.

13. AEROPLANE CO-OPERATION. Contact aeroplanes will be used at daylight to fix the positions gained by the infantry, in accordance with the principles lately practiced in this brigade.
    Flares will not be used. Infantry will be issued with yellow handkerchiefs. - These will be waived whenever an aeroplane sounds its horn. Yellow handkerchiefs will mean nothing unless waived.

14. COMMUNICATIONS. Separate orders will be issued later.

15. SYNCHRONISATION OF WATCHES. A representative from each battalion will report at Brigade Headquarters at 6.p.m. on Y Day to synchronise watches. Watches will be again synchronised at 1.hour before ZERO in assembly trenches. A representative from Brigade Headquarters will visit Battalion Headquarters for that purpose.

16. CARRYING PARTY. Officers Cmmanding 2/rd, 2/1st, and 2/2nd.Bns will be required to detail asmall carrying party for Vickers Machine Guns and Light Trench Mortars (numbers will be given later)

17. EQUIPMENT. All troops will be in Battle Order and carry
    170.rounds.s.a.a.
    4.sandbags.
    2.iron rations.
    1.Box respirator & P.H.G.Helme.t
    1.Verey Light.
    2.Bombs.
    Pick & Shovel
    Full Waterbottle.
    Aeroplane Signals.

As many wire-cutters as possible will be issued to the 1st.waves.
  20% of the men will carry "P" Bombs. S.O.S. Rockets will be carried by Company and Battalion Headquarters. Runners are to be lightly equipped and Battalion runners will not carry rifles.

4.

18. **LIGHT SIGNALS & COMMUNICATION TRENCHES.** Instructions regarding use of Light Signals and Communication trenches will be issued later.

19. <u>NOTES.</u>

(a) It must be impressed upon all units that they are on no account to halt because units on their flanks happen to be held up. The best way of assisting their neighbours on such occassions will be to continue their own advance.

(b) All commanders must be impressed with the mecessity of maintaining their direction and marching straight on to their allotted objective. With this object the ground must be carefully studied beforehand, landmarks noted wherever possible and compass bearings taken.

(c) No papers likely to be of value to the enemy will be taken over the parapet.

(d) Not more than 20 Officers per Battalion must take part in an assault,& a proportion of reliable N.C.O's must also be left behind

(e) Officers and Men will be particularly warned against retaining documents taken from prisoners as souvenirs Very valuable information may be lost by failure to send in all documents so taken, which should be forwarded to Brigade Headquarters at the first opportunity.

(f) The word "Retire" does not exist; anyone using it is to be immediately killed

ACKNOWLEDGE.

(Sd) Captain.
Brigade Major.
173rd.Infantry Brigade.

173rd. ARTILLERY BARRAGE TIME TABLE - ATTACHED OPERATION ORDER No:-25.

Time	Barrage	Infantry
Zero.	Barrage opens 150.yards short of enemy front line.	Infantry leave assembly areas and advance across "No Man's Land" close up to barrage.
± 0.2.	Barrage lifts 50.Yards.	Infantry Continues to advance.
± 0.4.	Barrage lifts a hundred yards into enemy front line - stays there three minutes and moves back 100.Yds every three minutes.	Infantry continues to advance.
± 07".	Barrage lifts to 100 yards behind enemy front line.	Assault of front line by 1st.Wave - 2nd.Wave advances close up to Barrage.
± 0.10".	Barrage lifts 100.Yards.	2nd.Wave advances
± 0.13".	Barrage lifts 100.Yards and forms a protective screen to Infantry during consolidation. This line will be the S.O.S. line.	Assault of 2nd.Objective by 2nd.Wave - Infantry mops up and consolidates 1st. & 2nd.Objectives.

SECRET.

173rd. INFRNATRY BRIGADE.

Administrative Instructions No.6 issued with
Reference to Operation Order No:-25.

TRANSPORT. Will remain as at present.

RATIONS Each man will carry two iron rations and a full waterbottle.
WATER   All necessary grenades, sandbags, &c., for the attack will
S.A.A.. be delivered to unit's Q.M.Stores.
BOMBS   Dumps will be established in accordance with the attached
&c.   schedule in accordance with arrangements to be made by the
Staff Captain; when established, units concerned will be
notified, and will take same over.
    O.C.2/4th.London Regt. will detail one complete platoon
as carrying party. This party will be earmarked ready to
report to Staff Captain as required. In addition O.C.
2/4th.London Regt. will detail 1.N.C.O. and 3.Men as
Guard for the Brigade Dump - this party will report to the
Brigade Storeman at T.23.d.9.4. when called for.

STORAGE OF All packs &c., will be stored at the present Q.M.Stores
PACKS.   Q.M.Stores must be prepared to move on Z ± 1.Day.

REPLACEMENT OF The quick replacement of Lewis Guns etc., is important
ORDNANCE STORES. Units will report to Brigade Headquarters at once any
deficiencies.

OFFICERS & OTHER Officers and other ranks not going into the attack will
RANKS.   remain in the transport lines - when any of these reserves
Officers are required, Brigade Headquarters will be informed

STRAGGLER POSTS. Straggler posts will be established at :-
    T.23.d.8.3.
    U.25.b.5.2.
    U.26.c.4.5.
O.C.2/4th.London Regt., will detail 1.N.C.O. (Sergt.)
and 8.Men to take charge of these posts.
    Instructions for this party will be issued from this
Office.

PRISONERS OF A Brigade Prisoner Collecting Post will be established at
WAR.   B.11.a.5.2. in charge of an N.C.O. and 2.Men to be detailed by
O.C. 2/4th. London Regt.
    Prisoners captured will be sent back with as small an escort
as possible. The N.C.O. i/c of the station will keep as
many men of the escort as he requires, and will send the
remainder back with a receipt for the prisoners handed over.

    When parties of 20 or 30 have been collected they will
be sent back to the Divisional Cage at MORY - B.16.d.4.2.
    Officer prisoners will be kept seperate from the men.

SALVAGE. As at present.

MEDICAL. Arrangements will be notified later.

CASUALTIES. The following instructions as regards reporting casualites
during the operation are issued :-
    The ordinary detailed casualty return will be rendered up
to and including 12.noon on the day before the assault,
after which a system of "estimated" casualty returns will
come into force.
This will be rendered twice daily to reach Brigade

2.

Headquarters at 12.noon and 7.p.m.
 (Estimated casualties however exceeding 10% of any
unit will be reported at once.
The following information regarding casualties will be given:-
 (a) Total estimated loss of Officers since the
    commencement of Operations.
 (b) Total estimated loss of Other Ranks since the
    commencement of operations.
All wires will commence "Total Estimated aaa" and the total
will be accumulative.
 At the termination of the operation, or as soon as a unit
is withdrawn from the line, an accurate return of the casualties
sustained during the preceeding period will be rendered.
 This return must give the dates covered, ranks, initials
and names of officers, and total numbers of O.R's killed,
wounded and missing.
 Accuracy is essential in this return.

        Sd (F.H.Garraway)

            Capt.
          Staff Captain.
      173rd.Infantry Brigade.

8th. June 1917.

173rd. INFANTRY BRIGADE.

AMMUNITION DUMPS.

	Map Reference	S.A.A. (Boxes)	Grenades Hand. (Boxes)	No.23. (Boxes)	No.20. (Boxes)	Very Lights.	S. O. S. Red.	S. O. S. Green.
Bde.Forward Dump.	T.23.d.9.4.	100.	100.	30.	5.	600.	50.	50.
Right Bn.	U.25.a.7.5.	30.	60.	16.	5.	150.	20.	20.
Centre Bn.	T.24.d.8.2.	30.	60.	16.	5.	150.	20.	20.
Left Bn.	U.19.a.5.9.	30.	60.	16.	5.	150.	20.	20.
M.G.Co.	U.25.a.4.8.	100.	-	-	-	-	-	-

WATER DUMPS

	Map Reference.	Quantity. (Tins)
Brigade.	T.23.d.9.5.	200.
Right.Bn.	U.19.d.7.2.	60.
Centre Bn.	U.19.d.8.7.	60.
Left Bn.	U.13.d.7.7.	60.

RATIONS.

	Map Reference.	Number.
Brigade.	T.23.d.9.4.	1.000.
Right.Bn.	U.25.a.7.5.	400.
Centre Bn.	T.24.d.8.2.	400.
Left Bn.	U.19.a.5.9.	400.

Battalions will supply details of M.G.Coy & L.T.M.B.under their command, with rations & water.

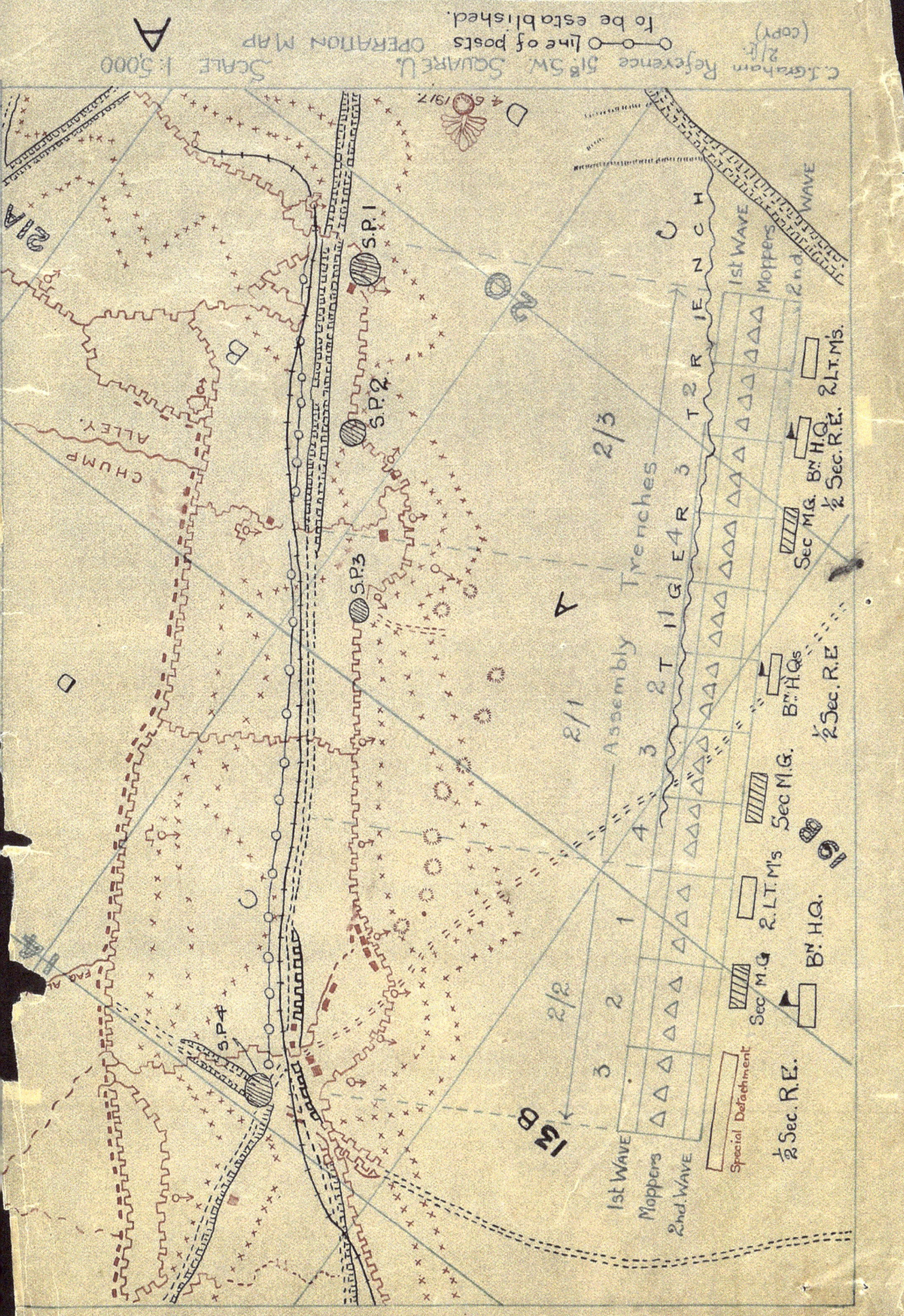

SECRET.   Copy No. 12

AMENDMENTS TO
173RD INFANTRY BRIGADE OPERATION ORDER NO 25.

10th June 1917.

Para 1. will now read:- PLAN.   The 173rd Infantry Brigade, supported by the 174th Infantry Brigade, is to carry out an attack on the HINDENBURG Front and Support Lines.
    The attack will be made by moonlight, Z day and ZERO hour will be issued later.
    Troops on our Right and Left will co-operate with rifle, machine gun and Lewis Gun fire, and will undertake minor operations as outlined in para 7.
    The objects of this attack are:-
        (a). To gain ground, to kill and harass the enemy.
        (b). To improve our tactical position.
        (c). To take prisoners.

Para 2. will now read:- OBJECTIVES.
            1st Objective.   HINDENBURG Front Line
    from U.20.b.40.17. to U.14.a.05.05.
            2nd Objective.   HINDENBURG SUPPORT LINE
    from U.20.b.45.72. to U.14.a.8.1.

Para 7. will now read:- SCHEME OF ATTACK.   The Brigade will attack with the 2/3rd Bn. London Regt. on the Right, 2/1st Bn. London Regt. in the centre, and the 2/2nd Bn. London Regt. on the Left.
    The 2/3rd, 2/1st and 2/2nd Bn. London Regts. will attack on a four company front.
    A Company from the 2/7th and 2/4th Bns. will be attached to the 2/3rd and 2/2nd Bns. respectively, and will be given the task of making good our flanks.
    The attack will be launched in two waves.   Moppers will accompany the first wave.
First Wave. of each Company, will consist of two platoons in single rank.   One platoon per Company will follow the first wave at 10 paces distance, to act as moppers.
2nd Wave will be 30 paces distance from the front wave and will consist of One platoon.
Special Moppers.   Light Trench Mortar Personnel, with three L.T.M.Bombs each, will follow the front wave to deal with dug-out shafts, which are near the Enemy's Support Line.
The Advance and Assault.   The whole assaulting force will move forward at ZERO and get close up to the barrage
Great care should be exercised:-

        (a). To maintain the distances laid down.
        (b). To lose no chance of reorganisation during advance.
        (c). To use compasses whenever a chance occurs; even when waiting a few seconds for the barrage to lift (This is vital).
NOTE:- The responsibility for the direction after the assault is launched lies with every man with a compass.
The First Wave. Will advance close up to the barrage, assault the first objective and push forward behind the barrage to assault, clean up and consolidate the Second Objective, dropping the moppers to deal with the situation in the first objective.   The special Moppers with the L.T.M. Bombs will follow the first wave to the second objective where they will deal with dug-out shafts as instructed in training.

2.

7. **Scheme of Attack** - continued:-

The Second Wave will advance at 30 paces distance from the first wave until after the first objective, when they will mop up the Sunken Road and any places between the first and second objectives. They will then push forward into the second objective and assist with mopping up and consolidation.

Para 8. will now read:- SPECIAL DETACHMENTS. O's. C. 2/2nd and 2/3rd Bns. will detail the Companies attached to them from 2/4th and 2/7th Bns. to form Left and Right defensive flanks respectively, as shown on Map

Para 9. will now read:- VICKERS MAXIM GUNS. The advance will be supported by the guns of the 206th; 198th and 214th M. G. Companies and the guns of the 21st Division.
O.C. 206th M. G. Company will arrange for two guns to follow the second waves of each Company of the 2/3rd; 2/1st and 2/2nd Bns. These guns will occupy the mebus positions in the first objective during hostile bombardments but will fire over the heads of our men in the second objective during a counter attack.
The remainder of the guns will employ indirect fire under orders of the O.C. 206th M. G. Coy.

Para 10. will now read:- LIGHT TRENCH MORTARS. O.C. 173rd L.T.M. Batty. will detail his personnel equally to the 2/3rd; 2/1st and 2/2nd Bns. to act as special moppers as detailed in para. 7. He will be responsible that they are handed over fully equipped.

                                       Captain,
                                       Brigade Major,
                                       173rd Infantry Bde.

Issued to Signals at:- ......

Copy No.
1. 2/1st Bn. London Regt.
2. 2/2nd Bn. London Regt.
3. 2/3rd Bn. London Regt.
4. 2/4th Bn. London Regt.
5. 173rd Trench Mortar Batty.
6. 206th Machine Gun Company.
7. 2/7th Battalion London Regt.
8. 110th Infantry Brigade.
9. 174th Infantry Brigade.
10. 175th Infantry Brigade.
11. Left Group 58th D.A.
12. 504th Field Coy. R. E.
13. "G" 58th Division.
14. "A" & "Q" 58th Division.
15. O. R. A.
16. G. O. C.
17. Brigade Major.
18. Staff Captain.
19. Brigade Signalling Officer.
20. Brigade Transport Officer.
21. Intelligence Officer.
22. War Diary.
23. War Diary.
24. File.

173RD BRIGADE AMENDED BARRAGE TIME-TABLE ATTACHED TO OPERATION ORDER NO. 25

ZERO	Barrage opens 150 yards short of first objective.	Infantry leaves Assembly Areas and advances across "No Man's Land" close up to Barrage.
+ 0.2	Barrage lifts 50 yards.	Infantry continues to advance.
+ 0.4	Barrage lifts 100 yards on to 1st objective, stays there three minutes and moves back 100 yards.	Infantry continues to advance.
+ 0.7	Barrage lifts to 100 yards beyond 1st objective.	Assault of 1st objective.
+ 0.10	Barrage lifts 100 yards.	Infantry continues to advance close to barrage.
+ 0.13	Barrage lifts on to second obective.	Infantry advances very close to barrage.
+ 0.15	Barrage lifts clear of second objective and creeps back to 250 yards beyond second objective at the rate of 100 yards every three minutes and forms a protector during consolidation. This will be our S.O.S. Line.	Infantry follows the barrage in at the double and commences to clean up. This must be done thoroughly.

"A" Form.
MESSAGES AND SIGNALS.

Army Form C.2121
(in pads of 100).

Prefix .... Code .... m.	Words	Charge	This message is on a/o of:	Recd. at .... m.
Office of Origin and Service Instructions.	Sent At .... m. To By		.... Service. Coby (Signature of "Franking Officer.")	Date .... From .... By ....

TO { 504 Field Coy R.E.

Sender's Number.	Day of Month.	In reply to Number.	A A A
* BM/1614	11		

Ref my order No 25 operation
is postponed for not less
shown three hours a.a.a. BM/153
as cancelled date + Zero hour
will be notified later

From 1/3rd Inf Bde
Place
Time 1-20am

(sd) G Graham 2Lt
for Bde Maj

Sent.

N.203/10-6-17.

O.C.
504 (WESSEX) Field Coy RE

The 504 (WESSEX) Field Coy. RE will be at the disposal of the B.G.C 1/3rd Infantry Brigade during the operations which that Brigade will undertake against the enemy at an early date. The R.E. will be employed assisting in the construction of Strong Points and carrying out any demolitions which may be required.

Please report to the G.O.C 1/3 Infy Bde, and find out what is required.

(Sd) E.M. Newell
Lieut Col. RE (T)
CRE 58th Division

10 June 1917.

Army Form C. 2118.

WAR DIARY
or
INTELLIGENCE SUMMARY.
(Erase heading not required.)

504 Fd Coy R.E.

Place	Date	Hour	Summary of Events and Information	Remarks and references to Appendices
ERVILLERS	12-6-17		**Work** No.3. Section. Constructing Shelters & Dug Outs at MORY COPSE.	
			" 4 " " " " " " "	
			" " " Advanced Bde. H.Q. & Special Shelters for pending Offensive Operations. R.H.	
			Special Party. Constructing Signal Office at (Suppt) Artillery Bde. H.Q.	
	13-6-17		**Work** As on 12th with the addition of parties preparing additional shelters for pending offensive operations. R.H.	
	14-6-17		ii Lieut. Row proceeded on leave to England.	
			Work Special Party constructing shelters for Signallers of Arty. Bde. H.Q.	
		10 am	**Operations** O.O. No. 30 of 14-6-17 received from H.Q. 173 Inf. Bde. – cancelling all previous orders – R.E. given no fresh instruction ⋕ Enquired of Bde. Maj. what was wanted of anything – his reply was to the effect that R.E. had been purposely left out of Orders so that they could be used in accordance with the new scheme of attack. ⊕	⋕ Order attached. ⊕ Correspondence attached. R.H.

All receipents of 173rd Infantry Brigade
Operation Orders NO: 30

IN Para. 4
    read 14th for 15th.

14/6/17

                                         Captain
                                Brigade Major,
                          173rd INfantry Brigade.

SECRET.   Copy.No.13.

173rd. INFANTRY BRIGADE OPERATION ORDER NO.30. 14 June 1917

Reference attached Maps:- BULLECOURT - 1/10,000 - 10.per Bn.
CHERISY 1/10,000
and Operation
    Map - A. Assembly Areas &   1. to each Bn to be issued later.
              objectives, 1/5,000 -

            B. Hump Position 1/2,500 - 250 to 2/2nd.Bn.London Regt.
                                 10 to 2/4th.Bn, "

            C. KNUCKLE position.
                 1/1,250 - A few to 2/3rd and 2/1st.Lon Regt.

Report Map. 1.General Map   - 100 to each Bn.
             2.Pigeon Map.   -   25 to each Bn.

173rd.Infantry Brigade Operation Order No:-25. dated 8th.June, together with amendments dated 10th.June are cancelled.

1. **PLAN.** 173rd.Infantry Brigade will attack the HINDENBURG front line on the 15th.June. ZERO hour will be notified later.
The troops on our right and left will co-operate with rifle machine gun, and Lewis Gun fire. The objects of the attack are :-
       (a) To gain ground & to kill & Harrass the enemy.
       (b) To improve our tactical position.
       (c) To take prisoners.

2. **OBJECTIVES** HINDENBURG front line from the Mebus at U.20.b.52.60. to U.14.a.05.05. and CROSS ROADS in U.14.c.

3. **ASSEMBLY AREAS** Units will move to their assembly areas by dark and will be in their alloted positions (See map A.) by -30.minutes. The greatest care should be taken to avoid unnecessary movement and noise forward of the RAILWAY EMBANKMENT. All movement into the assembly areas will be across the open. To avoid confusion guide tapes will be laid from the railway embankment by battalions concerned. All units alloted to either of the assembly areas will come under the command of officers commanding battalions concerned by 9.p.m. the 14th. June.

4. **ADVANCED BRIGADE HD QRS.** Will be established in the SUNKEN ROAD at T.30.c.3.9. by 10.p.m. on 14th.June. There will be a Brigade Report centre at U.19.b.9.2. this report centre will be used as Battalion Headquarters for centre of assaulting battalion. There will be runner posts at :-
       (a) U.25.a.75.50.
       (b) T.24.d.8.2.

5. **TIME TABLE OF ATTACK.** The attack will be carried out in accordance with table of barrages to be issued later. It must be clearly understood, however, that the times published are merely a guide to the infantry and are not orders for the exact times of assaults. It is of vital importance that the infantry should keep close up to the artillery barrage and advance whenever it lifts.

6. ARTILLERY SUPPORT.		The 173rd. Infantry Brigade will be supported by the artillery of three divisions the 7th., 58th., and 62nd.Dvvns. assisted by the V Corps Heavy Artillery.

6. ARTILLERY SUPPORT.
The 173rd. Infantry Brigade will be supported by the artillery of three divisions the 7th., 58th., and 62nd.Dvvns. assisted by the V Corps Heavy Artillery.

7. SCHEME OF ATTACK.
The attack will be carried out by one company of each of 2/3rd. 2/1st. & 2/4th.Battalions and 1½.Coys of 2/2nd.Bn. - detailed disposition and assembly areas are shown on attached map A1.
O.C. 2/8th. Bn. will establish a line of posts from U.20.b.40.16. S.E. along line of Sunken Road, connecting up with the existing posts R5, at U.21.c.2.3, and will detail one platoon to report to O.C. 2/1st.Bn, before noon on the 14th.June.
For the purposes of this operation the Companies of the 2/3rd. & 2/4th.Bns. mentioned above, will be under the orders of O's C. 2/1st. & 2/2nd. Bns, respectively.
Upon gaining the objective, companies will " Mop up " & consolidate under the protection of the barrage.
Battle patrols being pushed on to the line of the Sunken Road in U.14.c. & U.20.b.

8. DEFENCE OF CAPTURED OBJECTIVES.
In the event of enemy bombarding the captured line, the S.O.S. signal will be made, when our artillery will barrage enemy line with 4.5.Howitzers, and will place a strong barrage of 18.pounder 50.Yards short of the HINDENBURG Support Trench.

9. SPECIAL DETACHMENTS.
The company of the 2/2nd. Bn referred to in para 7. will advance and capture enemy strong points at U.14.a.15.00. and the Cross Roads at U.14.c.55.85.

10. VICKERS MAXIM GUNS.
The advance will be supported by the guns of the 206th. 198th. and 214th.Machine Gun Coys, and the guns of the 21st.Divn.
The O.C. 206th.M.G.Coy will place one section at the disposal of the O.C. 2/2nd. Bn. and one section at the disposal of O.C. 2/1st.Bn. These guns will accompany the assaulting troops taking up previous selected positions as soon as the objective is reached. O.C. 206th.M.G.Coy will confer with Bn Commanders concerned, as to the placing of these guns.

11. BATTALION HEADQUARTERS.
Battalion H.Q. for 2/1sy. & 2/2nd. Bns, will be at Railway Embankment in T.24.d.

12. AEROPLANE CO-OPERATION.
Contact aeroplanes will be used at daylight to fix the positions gained by the infantry, in accordance with the principles practiced in this brigade. Flares will not be used.
Infantry will be issued with yellow handkerchiefs. These will be waived whenever an aeroplane sounds its horn. Yellow handkerchiefs will mean nohing unless waived.

13. COMMUNICATIONS.
(i) Advance report centre will be at U.19.b.9.2.
Communications established b means of :-
(a) Wire.
(b) Power Buzzer.
(c) Visual.
(d) Pigeons.
(e) Runners

(ii) Telephone stations and relay post for runners will be established at U.25.a.75.60. and at T.24.d.8.2.
(iii) Power buzzers will be installed at advanced report centre and at a place in U.13.b. to be notified.
(iv.) A wireless station will be installed at T.24.d.8.2.
(v) Visual stations at U.19.b.60.85. - T.24.d.8.2. and T.30.c. 7.9. will be manned by 2/4th.Bn. London Regt. Signallers as at present.

14. SYNCHRONISATION OF WATCHES. A representative from 2/1st. & 2/2nd. Bns and 206th. M.G.Coy will report at Brigade Head Quarters at 8.p.m. 14th.June to synchronise watches.
Watches will again be synchronised at one hour before ZERO at the advanced report centre. A representative from Brigade Headquarters will be there for that purpose.

15. CARRYING PARTY. Officers command 2/1st. & 2/2nd. Bns will be required to detail a small party for Vickers Machine Guns (2.per gun.)

16. EQUIPMENT. All troops will be in battle order and carry the following:-
    170. Rounds. S.A.A.
    4. Sandbags.
    2. Iron Rations.
    1. Box Respirator & P.H.G.Helmet.
    1. Very Light.
    2. Bombs.
    Pick or Shovel.
    Full Water-bottle.
    Aeroplane Signals.
As many wire cutters as possible will be issued to the first wave.
S.O.S. Rifle grenades will be carried by Company and Battalion Headquarters.
Runners are to be lightly equipped and battalion runners will not carry rifles.

17. LIGHTS - SIGNAL. S.O.S. special rifle grenade bursting into 4 Red stars.
The ordinary S.O.S. signal will again be taken into use after 6.a.m. 17th.June. Resume normal rate of fire 2.White Parachute lights. These signals will be carried by each Company Headquarters.

18. NOTES.
(a) It must be impressed upon all units that they are on no account to halt because units on their flanks happen to be held up. The best way of assisting their neighbours will be to continue their own advance.
(b) All commanders must be impressed with the necessity of maintaining their direction and marching straight on to their alloted objective. With this objective the ground must be carefully studied beforehand, landmarks noted wherever possible, and compass bearings taken.
(c) No papers likely to be of value to the enemy will be taken over the parapet.

4.

(d) Not more than 4 Officers per Company must take part in any assault, and a proportion of reliable N.C.O's must also be left behind.

(e) Officers and Men will be particularly warned against retaining documents taken from prisoners as souvenirs. Very valuable information may be lost through failure to send in all documents so taken, which should be forwarded to Brigade Headquarters at the first opportunity.

(f) The word "Retire" does not exist; anybody using it is to be immediately killed.

(g) No reference to this Operation will be made over the telephone until after ZERO hour.

ACKNOWLEDGE.

(Sd)   Captain.
      Brigade Major.
173rd. Infantry Brigade.

173rd. BRIGADE BARRAGE TIME TABLE ATTACHED TO OPERATION ORDER No:-30.

ZERO.	Barrage opens 150.Yards short of objective.	Infantry Leaves assembly Areas and advances across "No Man's Land" close up to the barrage.
± 0.2.	Barrage Lifts 50.Yards.	Infantry Continue to advance.
± 0.4.	Barrage Lifts 100.Yards on to objective, stays there three minutes and moves back 100.Yards.	Infantry Continues to advance.
± 0.7.	Barrage Lifts to 100.Yards beyond objective.	Assault of objective.
± 0.10.	Barrage lifts 100.Yards.	Infantry Mop up and Consolidate objective.
± 0.13.	Barrage Lifts on to Main Support Line and remains till consolidation complete.	Infantry Continues consolidation, pushing out Battle Patrols to secure line of Sunken Road and Cross Roads in U.14.c.

SECRET.

To all concerned.

Reference para 17. 173rd. Infantry Brigade Order No:-30.

Delete sub-para referring to parachute lights, and substitute :-

" On S.O.S. Signal being made, our guns will place
protective barrage on, and 50.Yards in Front of
HINDENBURG support line. This barrage will continue
at varying rates of fire for 15.minutes. It will then
cease unless a further S.O.S. signal when it will
recommence and continue for another 15.minutes.

                          Sd - - - - - Captain.
                              Brigade Major.
                    173rd. Infantry Brigade.

14/6/17.

SECRET.

ORIGINAL ADMINISTRATIVE INSTRUCTIONS ISSUED WITH OPERATION ORDER 2B.
stands.

173rd. INFANTRY BRIGADE.

ADDENDA TO ADMINISTRATIVE INSTRUCTIONS NO:- 6.

Ref:- Operation order No:- 30.

RATIONS & WATER.

Rations and water for consumption on June 16th. for the Companies of the 2/1st; 2/2nd; 2/3rd; & 2/4th, Bn London Regiments established in the HINDENBURG Front line will be carried to ~~Headquarters~~ Company H.Q. in that line by carrying parties of the 174th. Infantry Brigade (10.Per Company)
O.C. Companies will arrange to send one guide per Company to U.13.c.5.2.
Rations and water for the Company of the 2/8th.Bn London Regt., will be delivered to Bn H.Q. and then carried forward to Company H.Q. under arrangements to be made by O.C. 2/8th.Bn London Regt.
Rations will be sand-bagged at transport lines of Bns concerned and will be taken by first line transport to U.13.c.5.2. except rations for 2/8th.Bn. London Regt.
Sandbags should be clearly marked showing Bns & Coys by a large letter - 2/2nd.Bn " A " - 2/4th.Bn " C "
1st.Line transport, Company Q.M.S. Carrying parties & guides will be at U.13.c.5.2. at 10.p.m. 15th.instant., and report to Staff Captain.

(Sd) F.H.GARRAWAY.
Captain.
Staff Captain,
173rd. Infantry Brigade.

June 14th. 1917.

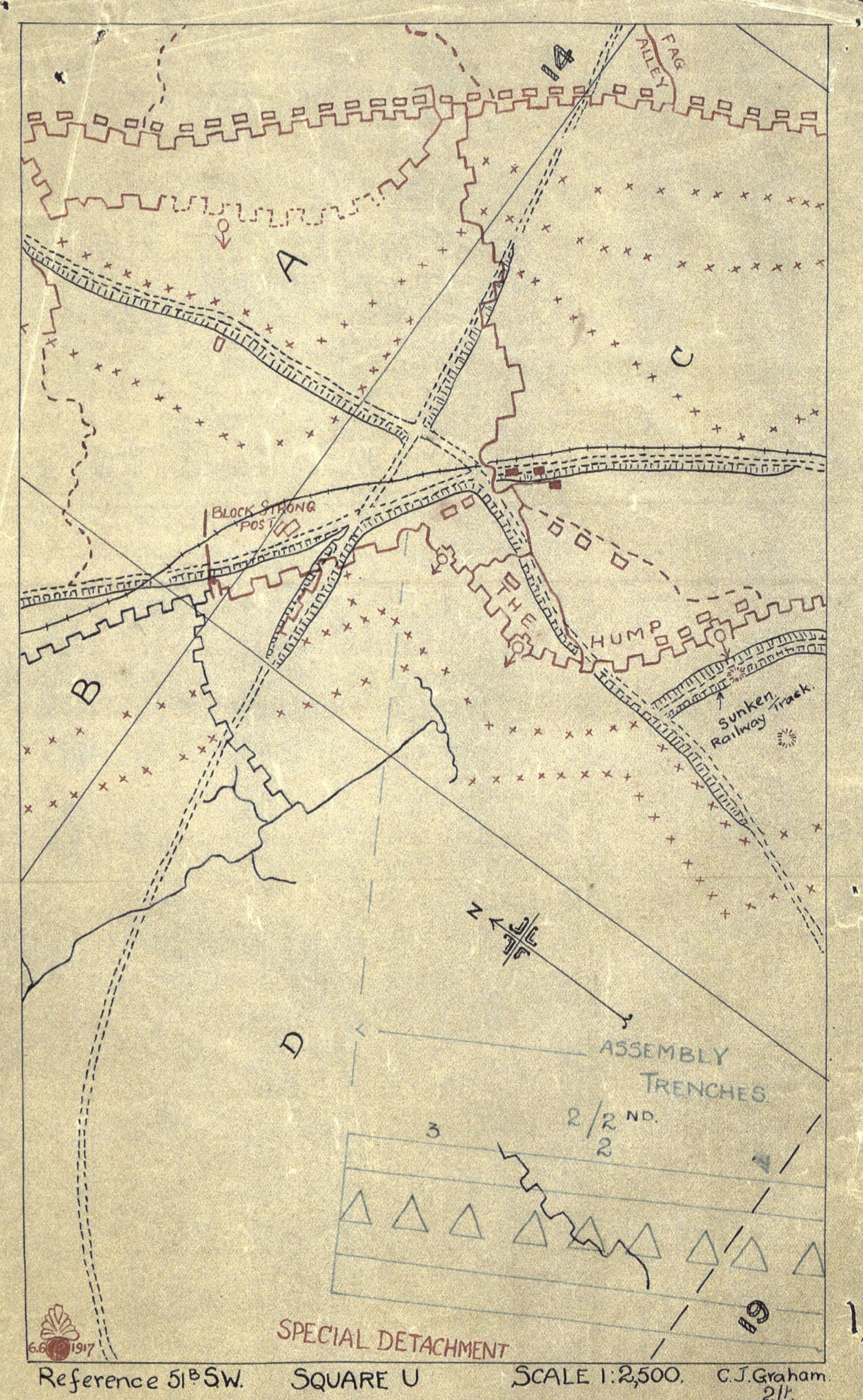

Army Form C. 2118.

504 Fd. Coy, R.E.

WAR DIARY
or
INTELLIGENCE SUMMARY.
(Erase heading not required.)

Place	Date	Hour	Summary of Events and Information	Remarks and references to Appendices
FRUILLERS	14-6/7	12 noon	Wrote to Pte Col & Sen 2de Maj - Arranged tour with the 30th Eng. Service be detailed as follows - Lieut V.G. Pearce & 15 O.R. from N°1. Section - Attached to 2/1st Bn Lond Regt.) for demolition parties & supervision of the construction of Strong Points & Trenches. " " F.W. Burnett & 17 " " " 2, " " " " 2/3rd " " " " " B.O. Armitage & 17 " " " 3, " " " " 1/2/2nd " " " Details of N°s 1, 2 & 3 Sections } In reserve at Coy H.Q. Camp. N° 4 Section }	
		6 pm	1 NCO & 2 Sappers from N° 3 Section join "C" Coy. 2/2nd Bn Lond Regt. as demolition party.	
		8 "	O.C. reports to H.Q. 173rd Inf Bde. for the period of the operations.	
		9.15 "	2 NCOs & 12 Sappers from N° 1 Section join "C" Coy. 2/1st Lond Regt. to provide demolition party to work Coy & supervision parties for Bn. 4 Sappers from N° 2 Section report to O.C. 2/1st Bn Lond Regt. to accompany the first of the attack for demolition work (O.C. 2/1st Bn Lond Regt. has a complete force drawn from 2/1st, 2/3rd, 2/5th Bns Lond Regt - with R.E. & T/M.B.)	

Army Form C. 2118.

WAR DIARY
or
INTELLIGENCE SUMMARY.
(Erase heading not required.)

504 Fd. Coy. R.E.

Place	Date	Hour	Summary of Events and Information	Remarks and references to Appendices
ERVILLERS	15-6-17	2.45 a.m.	Operations. Zero hour for attack in accordance with orders. Attack successful as indicated in Bde. O.O. No. 31 of 15-6-17. R.E. detachments apparently used to supervise consolidation as demolition work was not required except on our LEFT from which no report has come in - subsequent report that whole R.E. party "missing" on our LEFT.	# Copy attached
		10 a.m.	Lieut V.G. Pearce - 2 NCOs & 4 Sappers 1/No.1. Section arrive at RAILWAY EMBANKMENT to await orders from O.C. 2/1st Bn. Lond. Regt.	
		11 a.m.	Information received by Telephone from Brig. Gen. Cunliffe 173 Int Bde that we have occupied our objective in the HINDENBERG FRONT LINE & that he requires a communication trench cut from the HINDENBERG FRONT LINE on our LEFT (occupied for some time by 21st Divn.) through the Block to that part of the HINDENBERG FRONT LINE just occupied by us - Work to commence as soon as possible - Party for this work detailed as follows - Sergt. E.P. Spurlock & 19 O.R. of No.4 Section (no officer available) Lond. Regt. at 9 p.m. as work cannot commence till then.	
		2.30 pm	Sergt. Spurlock reports to Adv. Bde. H.Q. & is ordered to report to H.Q. 2/1 Bn.	
		9.0 "	Sergt. Spurlock reports to H.Q. 2/1 Bn. Lond. Regt. & proceeds to work as detailed above.	R.H.

SECRET.

Copy No.12.

173rd. INFANTRY BRIGADE OPERATION ORDER No:-31.

Reference Map Sheets - BULLECOURT 1/10.000.
- CHERISY 1/10.000 and A2.   June 15th.1917.

---

1. As far as can be ascertained, the situation at present is as follows. Our troops have captured and occupied the whole of this morning's objective with the exception of a small portion of the HINDENBURG FRONT LINE about the MEBUS at U.14.c.67.11. Orders have been given for this portion to be cleared up under arrangements to be made between O.C's 2/1st and 2/2nd.Bn.Lon Regts, In co-operation with us the 21st.Division on our left will assault the HINDENBURG LINE from U.14.a.45.45. (Exclusive) north-westwards. The boundary line between us and 21st.Division will be a line joining U.14.a.45.45. to U.14.a.00.15.(inclusive to us)

2. The attack will be resumed in the early hours of to-morrow, Zero Hour will be notified later. The objective will be the HINDENBURG support Line from U.20.b.50.70. to U.14.a.45.45., a defensive flank being formed along line U.20.b.50.70. - U.20.b.45.52. - U.20.b.50.60.

3. Assaulting Troops as shown below will be in assembly positions in HINDENBURG Front Line by 2.10.a.m. (MOONRISE) and O.C's concerned will report assembly completed to Brigade Head Quarters by using code word "BANANA"

    3.Companies, 2/3rd.London Regt   - 1.Coy.2/8th.London Regt.
                                         (Under O.C.2/3rd.Bn.)
    3.Companies 2/1st.Bn.London Regt.

    2½.Companies 2/2nd.Bn.London Regt.

    2.Companies 2/4th.Bn.London Regt. (Under O.C.2/2nd.Bn.)

    In addition each assaulting party will be accompanied by a proportion of L.T.M.Personnel with Stokes Bombs for dealing with Dug-outs and R.E. for assistance in consolidation and blocking of the tunnels known to exist underneath HINDENBURG SUPPORT LINE.
    All units alloted to either of the assembly areas will come under the command of Officers Commanding Battalions concerned by 9.0.p.m. to-day.
    Detailed disposition and assembly areas are shown on attached map.A.2.

4. Scheme of attack. The attack will be carried out in one wave supported by Mopper Up and detachment of R.E. and L.T.M. personnel mentioned above.
    The proportion of assaulting troops to mopper up will be 3 to 1.
    Barrage Time table will be forwarded as soon as received.

5. All posts in advance of HINDENBURG Front Line will be withdrawn by 3.a.m. Any alteration in localities selected for Bn.Battle H.Q. will be notified to Bde.Hd.Qtrs immediately.

6. The arrangements and instructions outlined in paras.4;5;6;13;16;17; and 18 of 173rd.Infantry Brigade Order No.30.of 14th.June will stand.

7. VICKERS GUNS The advance will be supported by the guns of the 206th., 198th., & 214th.Machine Gun Companies.
   O.C. 206th.M.G.Co. will arrange that 8.Machine Guns are in position and ready for action in HINDENBURG FRONT LINE as soon as possible after receipt of this order. No Vickers Guns will be sent forward of this line until further orders.

8. Contact Aeroplanes will be used at Daylight to fix the position gained by the Infantry in accordance with the principles practiced by this Brigade.
RED FLARES will be used also Yellow Handkerchiefs whenever an aeroplane sounds its horn or fires a White Very Light.
Yellow handkerchiefs will mean nothing unless waived.

9. Synchronisation of Watches. A representative of the 2/1st., 2/2nd. and 2/3rd Battalions, 206th.Machine Gun Company and 173rd. L.T.M.Battery will report at advanced Brigade Head Quarters at 7.30.p.m. to-day.
Wataches will be again synchronised 1.hour before Zero at the advanced report centre. A representative from Bde.Hd.Qtrs. will be there for the purpose.

10. Troops should be reminded that if shelled while assembling this will not necessarily mean that the enemy have discovered them.
In the event of severe casualties being experienced while assembling troops will push on to the HINDENBURG Front Line and reorganise there. In this case the whole of the garrison (Less Vicker's Guns) of this line will assault together at ZERO. Should such action become necessary Bde.H.Q. will be informed by the senior officer on the spot and arrangements will be made to ~~reorganise~~ regarrison the HINDENBURG Front Line.

11. ACKNOWLEDGE.

                                                Sd.   Capt.
                                                Brigade Major.
                                     173rd.Brigade.

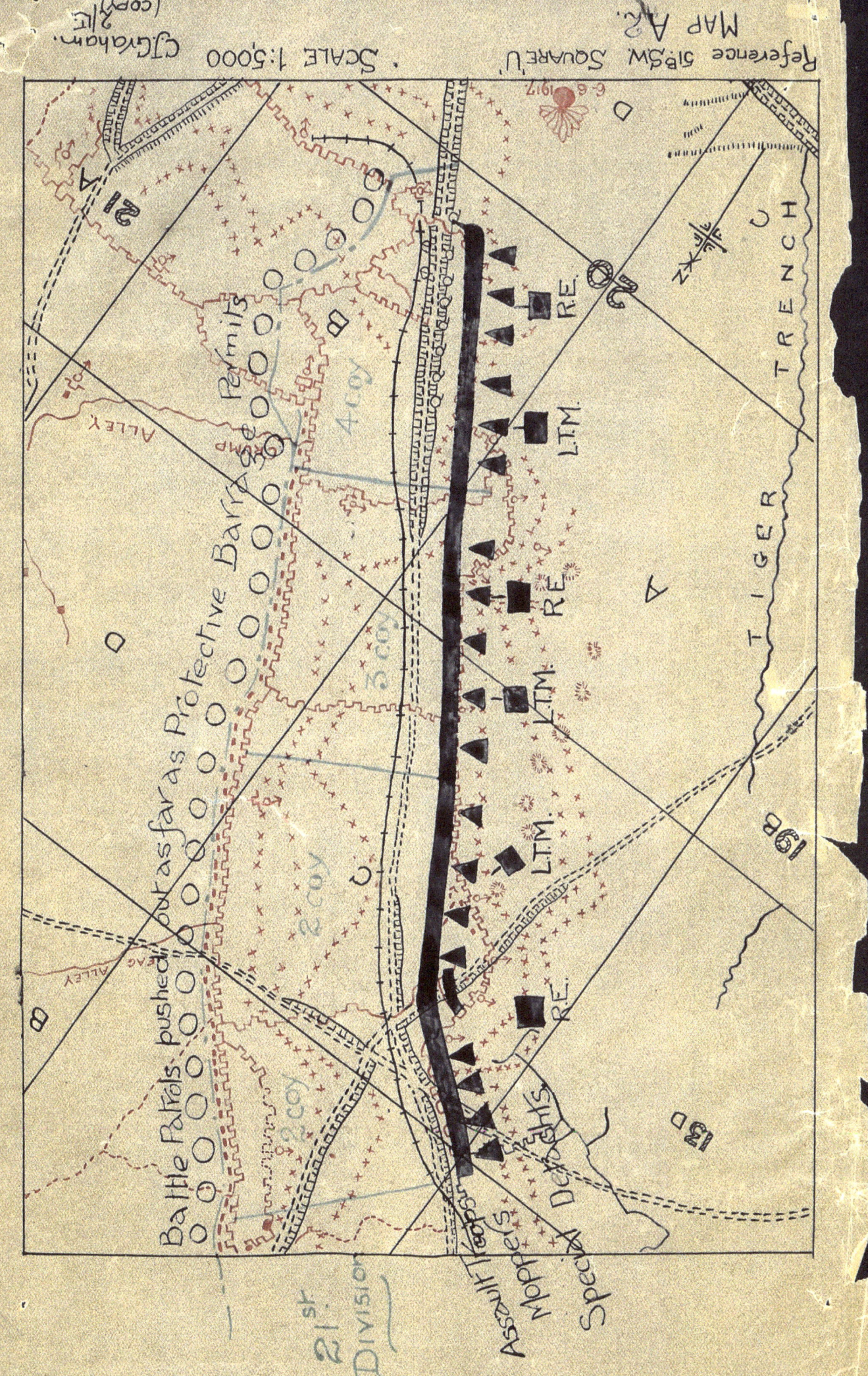

Army Form C. 2118.

WAR DIARY
or
INTELLIGENCE SUMMARY.
(Erase heading not required.)

504 Fd Coy, R.E.

Place	Date	Hour	Summary of Events and Information	Remarks and references to Appendices
ERVILLERS	15/6/17	9.0 pm	12 Sappers from No 3. Section join the 2/2" Bn Lond Regt. to accompany the attack made during the night 15/6/17 — 3 Sappers going with each Infantry Coy. to permit demolition work & supervision of consolidation.	
		10.0 pm	1 Lieut. J.W. Bennett, 2 N.C.O.s & 12 Sappers from No 2. Section join No 2/3" Bn. Lond. Regt. to accompany attack on HINDENBERG SUPPORT LINE.	
		10.30 pm	Sergt. Spurlock's party commences work after being delayed in getting to site (congestion of traffic in Communication Trenches)	
		11.0 pm	Lieut. B.O. Bunting in accordance with instructions reports to Battle H.Q. 2/2" Bn. Lond. Regt. in FACTORY AVENUE & finds the shelter demolished by shell fire & H.Q. shifted.	
			Casualties reported during this day :—	
			Killed. No 506491 Sap. ASHTON. H.	
			" 506516 " SCOTT. W.	
			Wounded " 506599 " BRITTAIN. E.	
			" 506449 " HUSSEY. J.	
			" 506512 " HOWELL. F.H.	

Army Form C. 2118.

WAR DIARY
or
INTELLIGENCE SUMMARY.

(Erase heading not required.)

504 Fd. Coy. R.E.

Instructions regarding War Diaries and Intelligence Summaries are contained in F.S. Regs, Part II. and the Staff Manual respectively. Title pages will be prepared in manuscript.

Place	Date	Hour	Summary of Events and Information	Remarks and references to Appendices
ERVILLERS	16-6-17	3.0 am	Zero hour for attack on HINDENBERG SUPPORT LINE.	
		5.45"	1st Lieut. J.W. Burnett, 1 N.C.O. & 4 Sappers of No. 2 Section reach the Battle M.P. of the 2/3rd Bn. Lond Regt. in the HINDENBERG FRONT LINE.	
		7.30 "	1st Lieut. J.W. Burnett attempts to make a communication trench from B.H.Q. 2/3rd Bn. Lond Regt. to SUNKEN ROAD – only 2 Infantrymen available for work – the Lt, 4 Sappers & 2 Infantry work till exhausted but unable to complete work.	
		4. pm	QM No. 506366, Corpl Ashton A. & 4 Sappers of No. 1 Section relieve Sergt. Spurlock's party.	
		6.30 pm	1st Lieut J.W. Burnett & No. 506052, 2nd Corpl. Bray R.C. proceed to the SUNKEN ROAD to make a Day Our Reconnaissance for the O.C. 2/3rd Bn. Lond Regt. Reconnaissance successful & Report made	
		7.0 "	Sergt. Spurlock's party relieve Cpl Ashton's party & resume work on the Left Flank communications.	
		8.0 "	Lieut. B.O. Bunting & V.G. Pearce report & are instructed to return to Coy. H.Q. Camp.	R.J.L

Army Form C. 2118.

WAR DIARY
or
INTELLIGENCE SUMMARY.

504 Fd Cy R.E.

Place	Date	Hour	Summary of Events and Information	Remarks and references to Appendices
ERVILLERS	16-6-17	6pm	Capt Tamlyn with 8 Sappers & 250 Corps Cavalry as working Party proceed to dig Communication Trench from PELICAN AVENUE to SUNKEN ROAD North of PELICAN AVENUE & extend in a N.W. Direction towards the extreme RIGHT of that part of the HINDENBERG FRONT LINE held by us. Special Party constructing shelters & Dug Outs for Brigt. Artillery during the period 14-17 June. R.W.A.	

WAR DIARY
or
INTELLIGENCE SUMMARY.

Army Form C. 2118.

504 Fd Co R.E.

Place	Date	Hour	Summary of Events and Information	Remarks and references to Appendices
ERVILLERS	17-6-17	2.45 a.m.	²Lieut. J.W. Burnett & party of No.2. Section leave the HINDENBERG FRONT LINE with No. 2/5th Lond. Regt. relieved by 2/5th Lond. Regt.	
		6.30 a.m.	Sergt. Spurlock's party complete task establish communication on the LEFT Flank — Total Length of trench made by clearing & sapping = 125 yards.	

		10.0 a.m.	Section officers' reports confirm additional casualties as follows —
			
			 Wounded No. 153919. Sap. YATES, F.
			             " 506438. " HOYAL, J.E.
			 MISSING No. 506162. Corpl. HATT, L.T.
			             " 183635. Sap. ABBOTT, A.T.
			             " 552662. " HEALEY, J.T.
			             " 506165 " FLETCHER, G.G.
			
			 All the casualties, (with the exception of Sap BRITTAIN) were suffered by the party which took part in the attack on the HINDENBERG LINE during the night of June 14 –15th. Sap. BRITTAIN was wounded on the 15th whilst working on LEFT FLANK COMMUNICATION	

Army Form C. 2118.

WAR DIARY
or
INTELLIGENCE SUMMARY.
(Erase heading not required.)

504 Fd. Cy. R.E

Place	Date	Hour	Summary of Events and Information	Remarks and references to Appendices
FRUILLERS	17.6.17	2pm	Information received that the 173 Inf. Bde. has been relieved by the 174 Inf. Bde.	
	3 "		O.C. Coy. reports to Brig. Gen. Cmdg. 174 Inf. Bde. & arranges for the supervision of construction of Strong Points in HINDENBERG FRONTLINE.	
	6 "		Maj. Jocelyn & 12 Sappers proceed to supervise construction of STRONG POINTS in the HINDENBERG FRONTLINE (part captured on 14–16.) Capt. Tamlyn, 8 Sappers & 250 Corps Cavalry proceed to work on the repair of the 16.t RH	

Army Form C. 2118.

WAR DIARY
or
INTELLIGENCE SUMMARY.

(Erase heading not required.)

504 Fd. Coy. R.E.

Place	Date	Hour	Summary of Events and Information	Remarks and references to Appendices
ENNILLERS	18-6-17	3 a.m.	Maj. Lockett & party return to Coy. H.Q. Camp - very little work having been possible owing to hostile activity.	
		8.30 "	Capt. Tarley & party return to Coy. H.Q. Camp - work delayed by breakdown of Light Railway conveying Working Party & tools to Ry. EMBANKMENT.	R.L.
	19-6-17	2 p.m.	Coy. hand over all work (except Special Putty work for Div. Art) to 511 Fd Coy R.E. & move to ABLAINZEVELLE.	R.L.
		7.0 "	Move to ABLAINZEVELLE completed	R.L.
ABLAINZE-VELLE	20-6-17		Coy. engaged in overhauling kit & stores.	R.L.
	21-6-17		Coy. engaged in Improving Quarters & Camp arrangements. Report on operations of 3/9 & 14/17 June made to C.R.E. #	R.S.L.
	22-6-17		Coy. 2 P.": with addition of Demolishing dangerous building (ex-Town Major R.H. attached ABLAINZEVELLE	#1copy R.L.
	23-6-17		Coy. 2.2. ": with addition of erecting Huts for Div. H.Q.	R.L.
	24-6-17		Coy. 2.3 "	R.L.
	25-6-17		Coy. 2.3 " Reconnaissance made of THIEPVAL - HAMEL Road. Information required that No. 506165, Sap. FLETCHER, G.G. previously reported "missing" is "Wounded not MISSING"	R.L.

Army Form C. 2118.

WAR DIARY
or
INTELLIGENCE SUMMARY.
(Erase heading not required.)

504 Fd Coy. R.E.

Place	Date	Hour	Summary of Events and Information	Remarks and references to Appendices
ABLAINZ -EVILLÉ	26-6-17		(i) Lieut. R. Row returns from leave. Capt. Tanlyn with 2 Officers & Nos 1 & 4 Sections proceed to HAMEL for the purpose of undertaking special road repairs on the HAMEL - THIEPVAL Road - working party of 500 supplied by 2/9th & 2/10th Bns. Lon. Regt. No 2. Section. working at Bde HQ. " 3 " . Improving Camp area.	R.F.L. R.F.L.
	27-6-17		Work as on 26.6.17	
	28-6-17		Lieut. B.O. Bunting proceeds to England on leave Capt. Tanlyn & party return to Camp on completion of work at HAMEL No 506260. Corpl. COOMBE. C. proceeds to ROUEN to take up the duties of Instructor in RE Field Work at Carpentry School for the period 1-7-17 to 31-8-17.	R.F.L.

Army Form C. 2118.

WAR DIARY
or
INTELLIGENCE SUMMARY.
(Erase heading not required.)

504 Field Co. R.E.

Instructions regarding War Diaries and Intelligence Summaries are contained in F. S. Regs., Part II. and the Staff Manual respectively. Title pages will be prepared in manuscript.

Place	Date	Hour	Summary of Events and Information	Remarks and references to Appendices
ABLAINZE-VELLE	29/6/17		Major Lockett proceeds to Div. Q. as acting to D.R.E. Capt Townley in charge of Company. Nor 2 Section shoring up Building for Town Major ABLAIZEVELLE. 3 " " Improving Camp area	WD/G
	30.		No. 4 Section continues work of No 2 Section 3 " " Improving Camp area	WD/G

R.S.Thornham? Maj.
O.C. 504 Fd Coy R.E.

1577 Wt. W10791/1773 500,000 1/15 D. D. & L. A.D.S.S./Forms/C. 2118.

Army Form C. 2118.

JR 504 Fd Coy R.E.

WAR DIARY
or
INTELLIGENCE SUMMARY.

(Erase heading not required.)

Instructions regarding War Diaries and Intelligence Summaries are contained in F. S. Regs., Part II. and the Staff Manual respectively. Title pages will be prepared in manuscript.

Place	Date	Hour	Summary of Events and Information	Remarks and references to Appendices
ABLAINZE-VELLE	1/7/17		Company improving Camp and erection of Buildings in same.	WD/T.
	2/7/17		D[o].	WD/T.
			2nd Lt. W.H.Shaddock admitted to Hospital (sick).	WD/T.
	3/7/17		Work same as 1/7/17.	WD/T.
			D[o]. D[o].	
	4/7/17		2nd Lt Row and 6 men to RUYAULCOURT taking over R.E. Dump and works of Companies of 42nd & 59th Divisions in back areas.	
	5/7/17		2nd Lt BURNETT and 10 men to NIEUVILLE BOURJONVAL taking over and preparing Camp of 469th Field Co. R.E.	
			Two men repairing Pump at Longpré Wood for Town Major ABLAIZENVELLE.	WD/T.
			Lt C.G. CUNNINGHAM attached to this Unit as per B.R.E.'s Order.	WD/T.
	6/7/17		2nd Lt Row and party at RUYAULCOURT checking materials R.E. DUMP.	WD/T.
			2nd Lt BURNETT and party at NIEUVILLE preparing Camp.	WD/T.

Army Form C. 2118.

WAR DIARY
or
INTELLIGENCE SUMMARY.
(Erase heading not required.)

504 Fd Coy R.E.

Place	Date	Hour	Summary of Events and Information	Remarks and references to Appendices
ABLAINZE-VELLE	7/7/17		Company inspected by O i/c. Washing Vehicles and packing Stores for move. 2Lt ROW & party at RUYAULCOURT checking stores R.E. DUMP. 2Lt BURNETT & party at NEUVILLE preparing Camp	2D/T
	8/7/17	2.0 pm	Company with Transport move to BANCOURT. 2Lt ROW & party at RUYAULCOURT checking stores R.E. Dump. 2Lt BURNETT & party at NEUVILLE preparing Dump	2D/T
BANCOURT.	9/7/17	6.0 pm	Company less Transport move to NIEUVILLE - BOURTONVAL. Transport move to YTRES. 2Lt ROW & party at RUYAULCOURT checking stores at R.E. Dump. 2Lt BURNETT & party at NEUVILLE preparing Camp.	2D/T
NEUVILLE	10.7.17		Sections 1 & 4 move to RUYAULCOURT " 2 & 3. improving Camp making Nissen Huts.	2D/T
	11.7.17		2Lt Ross hands over R.E. Dump RUYAULCOURT. R.E. services RUYAULCOURT, BERTRINCOURT and HERMIES roads. No 4 Section. making Stabling, D.H.Q. YTRES. No 1 Section improving Camp. " 2. Section improving Camp. " 3. Section preparing Transport lines.	2D/T
	12.7.17	9.0 am	Transport move to NEUVILLE - BOURTONVAL. (Continued)	#

Army Form C. 2118.

WAR DIARY
or
INTELLIGENCE SUMMARY.
(Erase heading not required.)

504 Field Co R.E.

Place	Date	Hour	Summary of Events and Information	Remarks and references to Appendices
NEUVILLE BOURJONVAL	12.7.17		Nos 1. Section. constructing Stables. B.H.Q. YTRES.	
			2. Sawing + transporting materials for water point NEUVILLE	
			3. Completing horse lines nr NEUVILLE.	
			4. R.E. services RUYAULCOURT, BERTRINCOURT and HERMIES	WDT
	13.7.17		Maj. LOCRAN returns to Coy. on return of C.R.E. from Leave.	RSh.
	14.7.17		Work on 12th "	RSh
	15.7.17		" " "	RSh
			Nos 1 & 2 Sections - Working on Water Points & trough standings.	RSh
			" 3 & 4 " - Camp Services & Hutting Scheme	
	16.7.17		Work on 15th. Nos 3 & 4 Section prepare to move to METZ* = Section Officers take on york	*Copy of orders attached
	17.7.17		move to METZ EN COUTURE	RSh
	18.7.17		Nos 1 & 2 Sections as on 15th.	
			Nos 3 & 4 " Improving & Repairing Trenches - erecting pole H.Q.	RSh
	19.7.17		Same as 18th "	RSh
	20.7.17		Same as 19th "	RSh
			Trench taped & dug by 173 Inf/Bde (No 4 Sect. supervising) to BOAR Co P.S.E.F. Capt. Tomlyn i/c.	RSh

Operation Order No:- 30.
by
O.C. 504 Field Co RE

Ref Map Sheet 57. c 1/40,000.

Sheet No:- 1.
15/7/17

Copy No 2

1. In accordance with CRE's Orders the Field Coy will be distributed as follows:-
   Coy H.Q. & No:- 1 & 2 Sections at NEUVILLE
   "   3 & 4   "   " METZ.

2. No's 1 & 2 Sections will continue work at YTRES & NEUVILLE - No:- 1 Section taking over the work of No:- 3 Section by 12 noon on July 16th.

3. No's 3 & 4 Sections will work in the 173 Inf Bde. Trench Area which extends from the RIGHT DIVISIONAL BOUNDARY (R.7.b.7.2.) to QUEENS LANE, exclusive (Q.5.d.8.1.) & will take over the work of the 511 Fd Co RE

4. The Officer & CO's of No 3 Section will be taken over the day work on July 16th & will be prepared to carry on on the morning of the 17th inst.

   The Officer & CO's of No. 4 Section will be taken over the night work on July 16/17th & will be prepared to carry on on the evening of the 17th inst.

   No:- 3. Section will leave a party to carry on present work until relieved by No:- 4 Section.

Sheet 2

(c) 2 Cyclists Orderlies

"C" Party   30 Cyclists

"B" Party
　　　　Advance cyclists leaves on 29th inst. and will report to Town Major ABLAINZEVELLE to ascertain billets & position of Supply Dump.
　　Party will move on 30th inst. to ABLAINZEVELLE.

　　　　Reveille　　　　5.0 a.m.
　　　　Breakfast　　　 7.0 a.m.
　　　　Hook in　　　　 8.15 a.m.
　　　　Move off　　　　8.30 a.m.

Head of party to cross starting point P.20.a.d.8. at 9.10 a.m.
　　Route via ROCQUIGNY, BAPAUME, BIHUCOURT & LOGEAST WOOD.
　　Move on 31st to FOSSEUX via AVETTE, ADINFER, RANSART, BEAUMETZ & GOUY, party to pass road junction immediately West of first C in COURCELLES-LE-COMTE (St. Lens 11) at 7.40 a.m.
　　Rations for 31st to be drawn at ABLAINZEVELLE on arrival on the 30th.

"A" Party   Sheet 3.
    move on 31st to FOSSEUX via
BAPAUME & SAULTY.
    Reveille   2.30 a.m.
    Breakfast   3.0 a.m.
    Parade   4.15 a.m.
Party (less Lt Pearce 4 horses, cooks cart
driver & 3 Batmen) entrain at P22.c.25.
at 4.30 a.m.
    Lt Pearces party will march to
BAPAUME station via YTRES, BUS,
ROCQOIGNY & LE TRANSLOY
    On arrival at BAPAUME party
of 100 men will be detailed for
loading vehicles & horses & unloading
at SAULTY as follows:—
    Lt Cunningham & Nos 1 & 3 Sections
will load & unload the horses &
vehicles of —
    Brigade Hd. Qtrs, Signal Section
2/1st Batt London Regt.
    Totalling - G.S. Limbers   12
              2 Wheel Carts   4
11 Lt Burnett & Nos 2 & 4 Sections will load
& unload the horses & vehicles of 504th
Fld. Coy. R.E, 198 MG Coy. 2/3rd Batt
Lon. Regt.
    Totalling G.S. Limbers   15
              2 Wheel Carts   2

Sheet 4

Lt Cunningham will report at BAPAUME to Bde Entraining Officer for instructions.

"C" Party under Sergt Tanner move on 31st by road to FOSSEUX via BUS, ROCQIGNY, LE TRANSLOY, BAPAUME BIHUCOURT, ABLAINZEVELLE, AYETTE, ADINFER, RANSART, BEAUMETZ, GOUY — Parades as for "A" Party

Stores - Vehicles
All section Stores including Blankets (less 2 Boxes per section) to be loaded & vehicles parked at NEUVILLE by 6.0pm on 29th inst.
Cooks Cart to be loaded by 3-45 am on 31st. 8 Section diaries to be carried on Cooks Cart & 2 Breast Ropes.
NO 1 Section will report to Capn Tamlyn at 2pm on 29th for dismantling huts & packing stores.
RATIONS unconsumed portion of days rations on days of travel to be issued before moving off & carried in the haversack, Water bottles must be filled.

Sheet 5

Waterproof Sheet will be carried folded in top of pack. Mess Tins inside.

(Sd) R.J. Lockett. (Maj)
O.C. 504TH FD. COY. R.E.

Copy ~~issued to~~ -

No 1	CRE
No 2	Captain Tamlyn
No 3	O.C. No 1 Section
No 4	O.C. No 2 "
No 5	O.C. No 3 "
No 6	O.C. No 4 "
No 7	File
No 8	War Diary
No 9	Spare.

Sheet 11

5. Sections will move on the 16th as follows
   No:-1. Section RUYAULCOURT to NEUVILLE
   " 3 " NEUVILLE to METZ.
   " 4 " RUYAULCOURT to METZ.
   Moves to be completed by 12. noon with
   the exception of the party of No:- 3 Section
   left at NEUVILLE who will move as soon
   as relieved by No:-1 Section.
6. Coy. H.Q. remains at P.22.d.2.3.
   Detachment H.Q. in METZ. will be at Q.20.d.3.1.

7. Completion of moves & taking over to
   be reported at once to Coy H.Q.

            Sd:- R.F. Lockett. Major
            O.C. 504 Field Coy RE

Copy No:-1 to O.C. No:-1 Section.
  "   " 2 " O.C. " 2   "
  "   " 3 " O.C. " 3   "
  "   " 4 " O.C. " 4   "
  "   " 5 " H.Q. 173. Inf Bdge ⎫
  "   " 6 " C.R.E 58 Divn.   ⎬ For information.
  "   " 7 " O.C. 511. Fd Coy RE ⎭
  "   " 8 " War Diary.
  "   " 9 " File.

Army Form C. 2118.

WAR DIARY
or
INTELLIGENCE SUMMARY.
(Erase heading not required.)

504 Fd Cy RE

Instructions regarding War Diaries and Intelligence Summaries are contained in F. S. Regs., Part II. and the Staff Manual respectively. Title pages will be prepared in manuscript.

Place	Date	Hour	Summary of Events and Information	Remarks and references to Appendices
NEUVILLE BOURJONVAL	21-7-17		Nos. 1 & 2 Sections: Water Points & Camp Services. " 3 & 4 " Repairing Trenches - night wiring & crestator M.D.	R.S.L.
	22-7-17		Same as on 21st.	R.S.L.
	23-7-17			
	24-7-17			
	25-7-17			
	26-7-17		Nos. 1 & 2 Sections as on 21st. " 3 & 4 Section - Repairing Trenches - night wiring & digging Advanced Posts.	R.S.L.
	27-7-17		Work as on 26th (excepting Advanced Post work.)	R.A.
	28-7-17		Work as on 27th All day work.	R.S.L.
	29-7-17		Work as on 28th	R.A.
	30-7-17		Nos. 1 & 2 Sections complete construction of Water Point. " 3 & 4 " returning to NEUVILLE. Transport proceeds to ABLAINZEVELLE under Capt Turlyn Work taken over by O.C. 90th Fd Cy RE.	R.S.L. *copy of orders attached
	31-7-17		Coy moves to FOSSEUX (by bus to BAPAUME - Train to SAULTY) Transport proceed from ABLAINZEVELLE to FOSSEUX.	R.A.

R Muscrah Major
O.C. 504 Fd Cy RE

Operation Orders
by
O.C. 504 Field Coy R.E.

Sheet 1
Copy No 8
No 2
28-7-1917

<u>MOVE</u> Company moves to FOSSEUX to
Quarters vacated by 63rd Fld. Coy. R.E.
The Company will be divided into
parties A, B & C as follows :—

"A" Party (a) O.C. Lt. Cunningham, Lt. Pearce &
  2 Lt Burnett
  (b) Dismounted personnel (less 14
      Brakesmen & 32 Cyclists)
  (c) 4 Batmen
  (d) 1 Driver (Cooks Cart)
  (e) Cooks Cart & pair of horses
  (f) 4 Officers Horses.

"B" Party (a) Capt. Tamlyn & 2 Lt. Row.
  (b) Mtd personnel less (1 driver
      cooks cart & 4 Batmen)
  (c) All Transport (less Cooks Cart
      & pair of horses, 4 Officers Horses
      & 30 Bicycles)
  (d) 8 Section Brakesmen (including
      6 Hd. Qtrs. " 1 R.A.M.C)

Operation Orders.   Copy No 8
by   Nos
O.C. 504th Field Coy. R.E   28/7/17

Reliefs.
The 504th Fld. Coy. R.E will be relieved by the 90th Fld Coy. R.E. on the 30th inst.

Section Officers will send to Company Office not later than 2- p.m on the 29th inst. all maps tracings, plans etc:- connected with work in the area.

Sections 3 + 4 will leave METZ for NEUVILLE on being relieved by party of 90th Field Coy. R.E. In case of non arrival of party they will leave METZ not later than 6.0 p.m. on the 30th inst.

Copy No 1 C.R.E   (sd) R. Lockett Maj.
"   No 2 Capt Tanlyn   O.C. 504TH FD. COY. R.E.
"   No 3 O.C. No 1 Section
"   No 4   "   No 2   "
"   No 5   "   No 3   "
"   No 6   "   No 4   "
"   No   " File
"   No 8 " War Diary
"   No 9   Spare

Army Form C. 2118.

WAR DIARY
or
INTELLIGENCE SUMMARY.
(Erase heading not required.)

504 Field. Coy. R.E.
Vol 8

Instructions regarding War Diaries and Intelligence Summaries are contained in F.S. Regs., Part II. and the Staff Manual respectively. Title pages will be prepared in manuscript.

Place	Date	Hour	Summary of Events and Information	Remarks and references to Appendices
FOSSEUX	1-8-17		Company re-fitting.	R.A.
	2 " "		" "	R.A.
	3 " "		Company less Mounted Section moves by Motor Buses to BOIS DES BOEUFS, TILLOY-LEZ-MOFFLAINS.	
TILLOY LEZ MOFFLAINS	4 " "		Reconnaissance made by Maj. R.J. Locatt of proposed work - viz - the reconstruction of EAST RESERVE TRENCH situated East of MONCHY LE PREUX.	R.A.
	5 " "		Work commenced at night. Work commenced on 4th.	R.A.
	6 " "		"	
			Cards of congratulation to gallant conduct received for :-	
			Nº 506676. Sergt. Spurlock E.R.	
			" 506392. 2" Corpl. Baker. C.	
			" 506670. L. Cpl. Grinchard. J.	
			" 506416. Sap. Pride. F.	
			" 506465. " Drewitt E.J.	
			" 506593 " Walsh. H.A. *	R.A. * Correspondence attached.
	7 "			
	8 "			
	9 "			
	10 "		Work continued on commenced on 4th	R.A.
	11 "			
	12 "			
	13 "			
	14 "		Work continued. Lieut. V.G. Pearce evacuated sick to Hospital.	R.A.

C.R.E. 58th Division No I/ 1475
HQtrs 58th Division No A 22/5240

C.R.E.

I am directed to forward herewith cards of congratulation for gallant conduct on the part of Officers and Men.

I am to say that the Divisional General takes the greatest pleasure in being able to put on record the fine behaviour of each individual concerned.

(sd) A.McNalty
Lieut Colonel
A.A. & Q.M.G 58th Division

5-8-17

2.

O/C 504th Field Co R.E.
~~O/C 511th Field Co R.E.~~

The C.R.E. has much pleasure in forwarding the enclosed cards of congratulation for gallant conduct in the Field.

He wishes you to personally express his thanks to all the N.C.Os and Men mentioned for their gallant behaviour and for their part in keeping up the reputation of the Field Cos R.E. of this Division and of the Corps of the Royal Engineers.

Captn R.E (T)
Adjutant 58th Divisional Engineers

6-8-17

Army Form C. 2118.

WAR DIARY
or
INTELLIGENCE SUMMARY.
(Erase heading not required.)

504 Fd Cy R.E.

Place	Date	Hour	Summary of Events and Information	Remarks and references to Appendices
TILLOY LEZ MOFFLAINS	15-8-17		Work continued & carried to a successful conclusion.	R.A.
	16 "		Lieut. C.C. Cunningham	
	17 "		" " R. Row	R.A.
	18 "		" " F.W. Burnett	
	19 "		Section Officers examined	
	20 "		Company moves into Rest at DUISANS, 4 miles West of ARRAS. Lieut. B.O. Burtin struck off strength from 10 July 1917.	R.A. ⊕ attached
	21 "		Company refitting - Message received from CRE⊕ 2/Lieuts N.H. TRERY & A.L. BARTLETT report for duty from 511th & 503rd Fd Coys R.E. respectively.	R.A.
	22 "		Company refitting	
	23 "		Company refitting	
	24 "		Company moves by road & rail to POPERINGHE & made to camp below - Coy HQ & Transport - 3 miles N.E. of POPERINGHE 2 miles N.E. of VLAMERTINGHE.	R.A.
POPERINGHE	25 "		Lieut V.C.P. Sayers with complete 1st strength of Coy. Most complete proceeded to ENGLAND & 2/trucks 1/strength of Coy.	R.A.
	26 "		Sappers employed on putting at SIEGE CAMP - West of VLAMERTINGHE	
	27 "			
	28 "			
EAST CANAL BANK, YPRES	29 "		Company moves to follow - H.Q. & Sappers to EAST CANAL BANK. North of YPRES - Transport to TOTEN HOEK FARM Camp.	*orders attached
	30 "		Reconnaissance made East of YPRES by Maj. Rocroft, Lieut Cunningham & Lieut Trery	
	31 "		Work commenced improving & clearing dug out lines on EAST CANAL BANK, making covered shelters in CALIFORNIA DRIVE, North of ST JULIEN	

R.Rocroft Major
O.C. 504 Fd Cy R.E.

C.R.E. 58th Division No. O.235

~~O.C. 503rd Field Co.R.E.~~
O.C. 504th Field Co.R.E.

      The C.R.E. 12th Division has written me a letter thanking your Company for what you did in his area. He says "Both Companies worked hard and well at a rather awkward job in a very exposed spot and both Companies worked by day and night. If they had not done it with considerable skill and care they would probably have had their work discovered."

I am very glad to pass this information on to you and I congratulate the Companies on the result of their work.

                                          Lieut. Colonel R.E.
21/8/17.   C.R.E. 58th Division.

Special Order
by Maj R. Stockert.
Cmdg 504 Fd Coy R.E.

Nº 1.
Sheet 1

Ref maps 1:40000 Nºs 28 & 51.C.

Move . The Company will move on the 24th to entrain at AUBIGNY for a new area.

Parade . 9 pm.

Dress . Marching order with waterbottles filled & ration in haversack.

Rations . All ranks must carry rations for two meals – one to be consumed whilst waiting at AUBIGNY. The other to be eaten as breakfast during the train journey.

Water . The Water cart will be filled at 7 pm. to enable men to fill their waterbottles – the water cart will be refilled on arrival at AUBIGNY STATION for use on detraining

Transport . Vehicles to be packed by 7.30 pm. under section arrangement.
Capt Tamlyn will supervise H.q. Section.
Capt. Tamlyn will be in charge of

Sheet II

all transport from 7.30pm till completion of move.
Transport to be at AUBIGNY STATION at 11.20 pm.
Capt Tamlyn will report to Brigade Entraining Officer at AUBIGNY STN. & will hand to him The Coy. Entraining State in duplicate.

23-8-17

R.W.Lockett, Maj.
O.C. 504TH FD. COY. R.E.

Army Form C. 2118.

WAR DIARY
or
INTELLIGENCE SUMMARY.

(Erase heading not required.)

50 4 Fd Cy RE

Place	Date	Hour	Summary of Events and Information	Remarks and references to Appendices
EAST CANAL BANK	1.9.17		Work. Cleaning, draining & improving CALIFORNIA DRIVE.	R.E.
	2 "		" Dug Outs on EAST CANAL BANK	R.E.
	3.9.17		Reconnaissance of the STEENBEEK by N.E. Row.	R.E.
			ii Lieut. N.H. TRERY to hospital - accidentally wounded.	
	4 "		Work same as on 1st. - in addition supervising Ruyper operation at HILLTOP FARM	R.E.
	5 "		Work as on 1st.	R.E.
	6 "		Same as on 2nd.	R.E.
	7 "		" "	R.E.
			ii Lieut N.H. TRERY returns to duty from hospital	
	8 "		Work as on 2nd. with addition of preparing accommodation in Concrete houses	R.E.
			in CALIBAN RESERVE & ST. JULIEN.	R.E.
	9 "		Work as on 6.	R.E.
	10 "		" "	R.E.
	11 "		" "	R.E.
	12 "		Improving & draining CALIFORNIA DRIVE	R.E.
			Erecting Elephant Shelters in ST. JULIEN	
			No. 1 Section proceeded to 55 Div. R.E. Wksps.	

Army Form C. 2118.

WAR DIARY
or
INTELLIGENCE SUMMARY.

(Erase heading not required.)

Instructions regarding War Diaries and Intelligence Summaries are contained in F. S. Regs., Part II. and the Staff Manual respectively. Title pages will be prepared in manuscript.

304th Field Coy. R.E.

Place	Date	Hour	Summary of Events and Information	Remarks and references to Appendices
EAST CANAL BANK YPRES	13-9-17		Work: Same on 12th with the addition of advice & assistance by No.2 Pioneer District & No.2. Sectn. to the Artillery Groups for the preparation of new battery positions – O.Ps. & shelters.	R.A.
	14"		Same as 13th:	R.A.
	15"		" "	R.A.
	16"		Same as 13th: – Forward accommodation in ST JULIEN now doubled in accordance with CRE's instructions by erecting 15 Elephant shelters each accommodating (crowded) 8 men = 120 men sheltered	R.A.
	17"		No.2. Sectn. Working for Arty. Group	
			"3 " " Repairing Bridges in YPRES CANAL.	
			"4 " " Increasing accommodation on EAST CANAL BANK. R.A.	
	18"		No.4 Section moved from EAST CANAL BANK to 58 Divl. R.E. Workshops.	R.A.
			"1 " " 58 Divl. R.E. Workshops in EAST CANAL BANK.	
			"2 " " work on 17th	
			"3 " " Improving accommodation EAST CANAL BANK & repairing bridges on 17th	
	19"		No.1. Section erecting Elephant shelters at CHATEAU VILLA & repairing CALIFORNIA DRIVE	
			"2 " " " on 17th.	
			No.3. Section improving accommodation EAST CANAL BANK R.A.	
	20"		Work as on 19th. Company in Reserve in accordance with OR OC No.26 of 17-9-17. A.A. (copy attd.) R.A.	

R.I. McGrath Major

Army Form C. 2118.

WAR DIARY
or
INTELLIGENCE SUMMARY.
(Erase heading not required.)

504th Field Coy. R.E.

Instructions regarding War Diaries and Intelligence Summaries are contained in F. S. Regs., Part II. and the Staff Manual respectively. Title pages will be prepared in manuscript.

Place	Date	Hour	Summary of Events and Information	Remarks and references to Appendices
EAST CANAL BANK YPRES	21/9/17.		Major R.S. LOCKETT left this station Capt W.H. TAMLYN taking command of Company. Work as on 20th.	WDH.
	22.9.17.		Work as on 21st. Congratulations received from G.O.C. 58th Division. Copy attached.	WDH.
	23.9.17		Work as on 22nd.	WDH.
	24.9.17.		Work as on 22nd. ✻ Congratulations of Field Marshal Commanding in chief received from G.O.C. XVIII Corps.	✻ Copy attached WDH.
	25.9.17.		Company moves to CALIFORNIA DRIVE. ✻ Letter of appreciation from G.O.C. 58th Division.	✻ Copy attached WDH.
	26.9.17.		✻ Lt Brenninkmeyer & part of Section I. & Lt Barry & "Lt Row taking Section VI " part of Section III acting improvements in conjunction with 175th Brigade	WDH
	27.9.17.		Company relieved by 475th Field Coy R.E. S.5.8.1.9. Company moved to Poperinghe 23. F. N.W.	WDH
POPERINGHE	28.9.17		Overhauling vehicles &c preparing for move	WDH

Copy.   XVIII Corps
         No. G.S. 66/216

The Field Marshal Comdr-in-Chief today
paid a personal visit to XVIII Corps Hd. Qtrs
to congratulate all ranks on their splendid victory in the Battle of 20th inst.

He desired me to convey to you his
high appreciation of the successful
attacks of the 51st & 58th Divisions. They
gained all their objectives advancing
close behind the barrage. They consoli-
dated their gains. They held their ground
in spite of several intense bombardments.

They were attacked by no less than ten
Prussian battalions at different times
between 3pm and 8pm. These counter-
attacks were all repulsed after fighting
at close quarters. The rifle & the
machine gun as well as the artillery
killed great numbers of Germans.

Our Heavy & Field Artillery deserve the
greatest credit for the accuracy of their
barrages & for the rapidity with which their
forward observing officers directed the guns
on hostile counter attacks.

I request that a copy of this letter
be sent to each brigade, battalion
and group commander who took

Copy
                                        G 1749

O.C. 504 Field Coy RE
etc

    The following from D.H.Q. is
repeated:—
    "The Divnl Comdr congratulates
all ranks on their grand success and
the magnificent and whole hearted
way in which they have carried out their
recent obligations."
    "All objectives have been taken &
the fine fighting spirit of the Division
has been nobly upheld."

                            (sd) J A Tyrrell
                                    Capt RE
                        Adjt 58th Div Engrs

22-9-1917.

in the action, and desire that all
ed so be informed that we have
ample evidence to prove that the
enemy's losses were heavy & that our
own were light.

(Sd)   Saml Maxey
                    Lt. Gen
22-9-   Comdg XVIII Corps

                2

To G.O. Corps H.Q/KE
    &c

        Forwarded & also
    Please inform all ranks as
    requested — of Corps Commander.

            Sd J.R. Diggle
                    2 Col RE
            A/Lt. Col Sur Engrs
24-9-1/

Army Form C. 2118.

WAR DIARY
or
INTELLIGENCE SUMMARY
(Erase heading not required.)

504th Field Coy R.E.

Place	Date	Hour	Summary of Events and Information	Remarks and references to Appendices
POPERINGHE	29/9/17	a.m. 9.30	Transport of Company under command of 2/Lt. Cunningham moved with Advance Party of 173rd Brigade in accordance with 173rd Brigade Order No. 42. Dated 26/9/17	173rd Bde O. No 42
	30/9/17	p.m. 2.0	Dismounted personnel of Company under command of Captain TAMLYN left for PESELHOEK Station to entrain in accordance with above order.	173rd Bde O. No 42

W. Tamlyn
Captain
O.C. 504th Field Coy R.E.

Army Form C. 2118.

WAR DIARY
or
~~INTELLIGENCE SUMMARY.~~
(Erase heading not required.)

504th Field Coy R.E.

Place	Date	Hour	Summary of Events and Information	Remarks and references to Appendices
LOUCHES	1/10/17	12:30 pm	Company arrived at LOUCHES	WDLT
	2/10/17		Company Training as per programme of Training	WDLT
			Do.	WDLT
	3/10/17		Do.	WDLT
	4/10/17		Do.	WDLT
	5/10/17		Do.	WDLT
	6/10/17		Do.	WDLT
			Capt. W.F.Tamlyn appointed 2nd in command of Company with acting rank of Major dated 22nd September 1917. ~~2nd Lieut~~ 2nd Lieut C.B. Cunningham appointed second in command of Company with acting rank of Captain. dated 22nd September 1917. (Authority Routine Orders No. 19. by C.R.E. 38th Divn. dated 6/10/17.)	MOST
	7/10/17		Reconnaissance of Billetts NORDAUSQUE for hutting by Major Tamlyn.	MOST
	8/10/17		Company Training as per programme	WDLT
			Do.	WDLT

Army Form C. 2118.

WAR DIARY
or
INTELLIGENCE SUMMARY.
(Erase heading not required.)

509 Fd Coy. R.E.

Place	Date	Hour	Summary of Events and Information	Remarks and references to Appendices
LOUCHES.	8/10/17	1 pm	Transport of Company under ii Lt ROW left for new area.	WDT.
	9/10/17	11 am	Company proceeded by Bus to new area. Capt C.C. CUNNINGHAM admitted to CORPS REST STATION. LICQUES.	WDT.
HOSPITAL FARM CAMP. R/Sheet 28. N.W. B.19.d.3.4	10/10/17		Nos 1.2 + 4 Lectures. Erecting Nissen huts. No. 3. Section. Camp services. Reconnaissance of contemplated work by O/C. ii Lt BURNETT reconnoitres huit on expiration of leave.	WDT.
	11/10/17		Nos 1, 3 + 4 Lectures. Erecting Nissen Huts. No. 2 section. erecting horse trainings.	WDT.
	12/10/17		Do	Capt C.C. CUNNINGHAM discharged from 19th Corps Rest Station. WDT
	13/10/17		Do	WDT.
	14/10/17		Major TAMLYN proceeded on leave to England. Command of Company handed over to ii Lt ROW. 13/10/17	WDT

Army Form C. 2118.

WAR DIARY
or
INTELLIGENCE SUMMARY.
(Erase heading not required.)

504th Fd Coy R.E.

Instructions regarding War Diaries and Intelligence Summaries are contained in F. S. Regs., Part II. and the Staff Manual respectively. Title pages will be prepared in manuscript.

Place	Date	Hour	Summary of Events and Information	Remarks and references to Appendices
HOSPITAL FARM CAMP. Pt Sht 28.NW. B3a.d.3-2.	15/10/17		Nos. 1-2-3+4 Sections. Erecting Horse Standings	PWM
	16/10/17		Do.	PM
	17/10/17		Do.	PM
	18/10/17		Do.	PM
	19/10/17		Do.	PM
	20/10/17		Do.	PM
	21/10/17		Capt. C.C. CUNNINGHAM reported for duty and took over command of Coy from II Lt. ROW.	PM
			Nos. 1, 2, 3, & 4 Sections. Erecting Horse Standings	
	22/10/17		Do.	ccc
	23/10/17		Do.	ccc
	24/10/17		Preparing for move. Packing vehicles etc.	ccc
MURAT FARM B30a82	25/10/17		Company less transport, moved to Map Ref. 28.N.W. B30a 8.2. in accordance with C.R.E's O.O. No. 30. Dated 24/10/17.	ccc
			i Lt ROW with C.R.E making reconnaissance of proposed work at RETOUR CROSS ROADS. V25.F.4.3. +	ccc
			ii Lt BURNETT with section attached to 173rd Inf. Brigade for work in connection with Operations.	

Army Form C. 2118.

WAR DIARY
or
INTELLIGENCE SUMMARY.
(Erase heading not required.)

504th Field Coy. R.E.

Place	Date	Hour	Summary of Events and Information	Remarks and references to Appendices
MURAT FARM B.30.a.8.2	26/10/17		Sections 1, 3 & 4 constructing track for Decauville railway at: Map Ref. V19.c.6.1. POELCAPPELLE. V19.c.6.1. Lt BURNETT & Section returned to Company H.Q.	
	27/10/17		546802. Sapper. ENGLISH. J. wounded in the thigh. Command of Company handed over to Major. W.H. TAMLYN on return from leave. Sections 1, 3 & 4. constructing track for Decauville Railway to new Gun positions. Sheet Map Ref. POELCAPELLE. V.19.C.6.1. 496853 Section. 2. MURAT FARM. Drainage of Company Camp Site. Sapper. HIDOR. A. wounded in stomach. Congratulatory Message received G.O.C. 5th Army. *	* Copy attached
	28/10/17		In accordance with O.R.E. 55th Divn Order No. W5/355. Section placed at disposal of Brigade Groups R.F.A. for work as follows. No. 1. Section " A. Group. " 2 " " B " " 3 " " C " " 4 " " D " Major TAMLYN attending at above Groups Headquarters arranging details of work to be carried out.	

Copy

To
OC 504th Fld Coy
etc

The following message from 58th
Division is repeated for information
"G.622. 26th Following message from Gen
Gough for your information a.a.a. Please
convey to all ranks engaged in today's
operations my very great appreciation of their
gallant efforts a.a.a. They have my sincere
sympathy as no troops could have had
to face worse conditions of mud than they
have had to face owing to the sudden
downpour of rain this morning a.a.a.
No troops could have done more than our
men did today and given a fair
chance I have every confidence in their
complete success every time"

sd. W Hidde Kelly
Lt Col RE
CRE 58th Division

27-10-17

Army Form C. 2118.

WAR DIARY
or
INTELLIGENCE SUMMARY.
(Erase heading not required.)

504 Field Coy R.E.

Place	Date	Hour	Summary of Events and Information	Remarks and references to Appendices
MURAT FARM.	29/10/17		Work as on 28.10.17.	20/17.
	30/10/17		Do.	70/17.
	31/10/17		Do. Capt. C.C. CUNNINGHAM admitted to Hospital	20/17.

WR Tamlyn
Major.
31/10/17. O.C. 504 F.C. R.E.

WAR DIARY
or
INTELLIGENCE SUMMARY.

(Erase heading not required.)

Army Form C. 2118

50th Field Coy R.E.

Vol 11

Place	Date	Hour	Summary of Events and Information	Remarks and references to Appendices

MURAT FARM.	1/11/17		In accordance with R.E. instructions continue at disposal of Brigade Groups R.F.A. for work as follows:-
			 No.1 Section . . A. Group
			    2 " . . B "
			    3 " . . C "
			    4 " . . D "
				* Copy attached.

	2/11/17		Congratulatory message received from General Officer commanding 3rd Army. Work as on the 1/11/17.	* Copy attached.
	3/11/17		Do. Do. Congratulatory Message from G.O.C. XVIII Corps.	WDT.
	4/11/17		Work as on the 1/11/17. No. 506416 2. Corpl. PRIDE.F. Shell wounds in buttock.	WDT.
	5/11/17		Work as on the 1/11/17. No. 576522 Sapper BATEMAN.T.F. Shell wound in head.	WDT.
	6/11/17		Company rested in accordance with instructions of C.R.E.	WDT.

Copy   QA/50.

173rd Inf Bde.

The following is an extract from a letter received by me to-day from Lieut General Sir Ivor Maxse K.C.B., C.V.O. D.S.O., Commanding XVIII Corps, and should be distributed for the information of all ranks.

1st November, 1917.

"To-day I have been so busy handing over that I could not make an opportunity of calling personally upon you and your Brigadiers to express to them and to all ranks my appreciation of the splendid work they have put in throughout the months they have been in this Corps. Their spirit has been magnificent throughout. On the 20th September they won the best battle yet fought in this Corps — and we have had 13 battles in Flanders. I consider the 20th September as the Red Letter Day of the Corps and the capture of WURST FARM was a real feat of arms — even in this war. Having captured this ridge the 58th Division not only held their ground, but they defeated no less than five Hun battalions which counter attacked them during the afternoon. They and the 51st Division were highly tried on that day, and the enemy was so beaten that he has never once counter-attacked us in strength since that date. I beg you will convey to your people how greatly I have appreciated their services and how sincerely I bid them farewell."

(Signed) A B E Cator
Major General
Commanding 58th Division

2/11/17.

Copy. C.R.E. 58th Divn. 9/1965
                d/d 1/11/17

O.C. 504th F. Co. R.E.

The following wire from 58th Divn is repeated for information:-

G.122 31st
"Following message from Gen GOUGH is repeated for information aaa begins aaa Please convey to the officers and men of the 63rd & 58th Divisions engaged in yesterday's operations my thanks and great appreciation for their gallant effort aaa Nothing but the impossibility of crossing the mud prevented their usual complete success"

(sd) W Hyde Kelly
Lt-Col. R.E.
C.R.E. 58th Division

Army Form C. 2118.

504th Field Coy R.E.

WAR DIARY
or
INTELLIGENCE SUMMARY.
(Erase heading not required.)

Instructions regarding War Diaries and Intelligence Summaries are contained in F. S. Regs., Part II. and the Staff Manual respectively. Title pages will be prepared in manuscript.

Place	Date	Hour	Summary of Events and Information	Remarks and references to Appendices
MURAT FARM.	7/11/17		Work as in the 1/11/17	WD↑.
	8/11/17		D⁰.	WD↑.
	9/11/17		D⁰ for Lectures 3 & 4. CAPELLE on Camouflage screen	WD↑. TOEL—
	10/11/17		D⁰.	WD↑.
	11/11/17		D⁰. ARTILLERY proceeded to V Army Infantry School, TOOTINGBURT.	WD↑.
	12/11/17		D⁰.	WD↑.
	13/11/17		D⁰. Warning Order N° 3. by C.R.E. 58 Div.	WD↑.
	14/11/17		D⁰. Operation Order N° 31. by C.R.E. 58th Div. WD↑ Reconnaissance of work in transmission trenches.	WD↑.
			O/c 504th Field C⁰ R.E. meeting O/c 20th Field C⁰ R.E. & 2 Officers from same unit. run by O/c 20th Field C⁰ R.E. rendered to O/c 20th Field C⁰ R.E. Work as on the 14/11/17.	
	15/11/17		Company Cyclists move to PORTLAND CAMP in accordance with Operation Order. N° 31. C.R.E. Work as on the 14th inst.	WD↑.

Army Form C. 2118.

WAR DIARY
or
INTELLIGENCE SUMMARY.

(Erase heading not required.)

504 Field Coy R.E.

Place	Date	Hour	Summary of Events and Information	Remarks and references to Appendices
MURAT FARM.	16/11/17	a.m. 10.30	Standing by ready to S/O 20th Div for R.E. Company move to PORTLAND CAMP. Sheet 19. S.E. X.23.a.2.9.	WDST
PORTLAND CAMP.	17/11/17		Company employed on Camp Services & erection of Nissen Huts at PORTLAND CAMP.	WDST
	18/11/17	a.m. 9-0	Company resting. Cleaning for temporary accommodation. No.1 Section under Lieut BARTLETT proceeded to INTERNATIONAL CORNER and reported to 3.E.S. XII Corps for work in accordance with instructions of C.R.E. 58th Division. Lt L.B. POWELL reported power reinforcement.	WDST
	19/11/17		Reconnaissance of Camps building scheme by O/C. Sections started on works as follows:- No. 2 Section. PUTLOWE CAMP. No. 3 " PILCH CAMP. " 4 " POUNDON CAMP	WDST
	20.11.17		Work as on the 19th inst.	WDST
	21.11.17		Work as on the 19th inst. No. 2 Section working at PETWORTH CAMP in addition. 1 N.C.O. + 3 men report to 173 Bde H.Q. as advance party for move to new area.	WDST

Army Form C. 2118.

504th Field Coy R.E.

WAR DIARY
or
INTELLIGENCE SUMMARY.
(Erase heading not required.)

Instructions regarding War Diaries and Intelligence Summaries are contained in F. S. Regs., Part II. and the Staff Manual respectively. Title pages will be prepared in manuscript.

Place	Date	Hour	Summary of Events and Information	Remarks and references to Appendices
PORTLAND CAMP	22/11/17		Work as on the 21st Nov.	WD+T.
	23/11/17		Work as on the 23rd inst. No 1 Section Transport returned from XIX Corps.	WD+T.
	24/11/17	a.m 8.15	Transport of Company proceeded by march route to new area. Sections railing vehicles preparing for move.	WD+T.
	25/11/17	a.m 10.0	Company moved by march route to PROVEN area and entrained for WIZERNES. Preceded by route march to JANETTE meeting Transport at WNW.	WD+T.
JANETTE	26/11/17	a.m 10.17	Company proceeded by march route to COLEMBERT.	WD+T.
COLEMBERT	27/11/17		Company employed improving accommodation, overhauling vehicles.	WD+T.
	28/11/17		Do.	WD+T.
	29/11/17		Do.	WD+T.
	30/11/17		Company Training Programme submitted to C.R.E.	WD+T.

A 5834 Wt. W4973/M687 750,000 8/16 D. D. & L. Ltd. Forms/C.2118/13

Army Form C. 2118.

WAR DIARY
INTELLIGENCE SUMMARY.
(Erase heading not required.)

Vol 12

Place	Date	Hour	Summary of Events and Information	Remarks and references to Appendices
COLEM-BERT.	1/12/17		Company training in accordance with programme approved by G.P.G.	2/Lt.
	2/12/17		do.	do.
	3/12/17		do.	1/Lt.
	4/12/17		do.	1/Lt.
	5/12/17		do.	1/Lt.
	6/12/17		do.	1/Lt.
	7/12/17	a.m. 9.30	Transport of Company moved to SAMETTE (Saying Area) in existence with 173 Infantry Brigade. Administrative Instrn. Nr. 20. dated 5/12/17	2/Lt.
	8/12/17	9.30	Dismounted personnel of Company moved to SAMETTE in accordance with	

Army Form C. 2118.

WAR DIARY
of
INTELLIGENCE SUMMARY.
(Erase heading not required.)

Instructions regarding War Diaries and Intelligence Summaries are contained in F. S. Regs., Part II. and the Staff Manual respectively. Title pages will be prepared in manuscript.

Place	Date	Hour	Summary of Events and Information	Remarks and references to Appendices
SAMETTE	9/12/17	a.m. 3.0.	Dismounted personnel of Company march to WIZERNES and entrained for ELVERDINCHE. Retrained and marched to Billets CANAL BANK. Sheet 28. N.W. C.13.c.0.7.	WD 1.
CANAL BANK. WEST.	10/12/17		Transport of Company arrive at MURAT FARM. Sheet 28. N.W. B.30.a.8.2. Reconnaissance of Work by O/C with O/C 204th Field Co. R.E. Taking over Dumps Tools in hand:	WD 1.
	11/12/17		Sections working as follows:- No 1 Section. Work at C.R.E. HdQrs. & Motor Garage D.H.Q. 2 " Work at CADDY TRENCH. 3 " Manning Pumps Trunk at RAILWAY COTTAGE. 4 " Work on forward BATTERY positions.	WD 1.
	12/12/17		No. 1 Section. Erecting Horse Standings at MURAT CAMP. 2 " do on the 11/12/17 3 " do do 4 " do do	WD 1.

Army Form C. 2118.

WAR DIARY
INTELLIGENCE SUMMARY.
(Erase heading not required.)

Instructions regarding War Diaries and Intelligence Summaries are contained in F. S. Regs., Part II. and the Staff Manual respectively. Title pages will be prepared in manuscript.

Place	Date	Hour	Summary of Events and Information	Remarks and references to Appendices
CANAL BANK WEST.	13/12/17		No. 1 Section. Party at forward Battery positions. Party at MURAT CAMP, work on Horse Trainings.	
			2 " " " " " " the 12th inst	
			3 " " " " " " do.	
			4 " " " " " " do.	INT.
	14/12/17		No. 1 Section. Party at forward Battery positions. Party at D.H.Q. Work on Garage.	
			2 " " " " " " the 13 inst	
			3 " " " " " " do.	
			4 " " " " " " do.	INT.
	15/12/17		Work as on the 14/12/17.	INT.
	16/12/17		do. 15/12/17	INT.
	17/12/17		do. 16/12/17	INT.

A 5834 Wt. W4973/M687 750,000 8/16 D. D. & L. Ltd. Forms/C.2118/13.

Army Form C. 2118.

WAR DIARY
or
INTELLIGENCE SUMMARY.

(Erase heading not required.)

Instructions regarding War Diaries and Intelligence Summaries are contained in F. S. Regs., Part II. and the Staff Manual respectively. Title pages will be prepared in manuscript.

Place	Date	Hour	Summary of Events and Information	Remarks and references to Appendices
CANAL BANK. WEST.	18/12/17		Sections 1 & 2 on forward Battery positions " 3. manning Dumps & trek area work " 4 GADDIE CAMP & TURCO FARM. " " Lt. N.H.TRERY returned their from Course of Instruction - FLEXICOURT.	20Lt.
	19/12/17		Sections 1.2 & 3 as on the 18/12/17. Section 4. Work on GADDIE TRENCH.t. Horse Standings BOUNDARY ROAD & ADMIRALS ROAD	20Lt.
	20/12/17		Work as on the 19/12/17.	20Lt.
	21/12/17		Do. Do.	20Lt.
	22/12/17		Do. Do.	20Lt.
	23/12/17		Do. Do.	20Lt.
	24/12/17		Do. Do. No.422791. Sapper KELLY. W. wounded.	20Lt.
	25/12/17		Section 1. manning Dumps; and trek area work " 2 & 3 Work on forward Battery positions " 4 Work at BOUNDARY ROAD & ADMIRALS ROAD.	20Lt.

Army Form C. 2118.

WAR DIARY
or
INTELLIGENCE SUMMARY.
(Erase heading not required.)

604th F.D. COY. R.E.

Place	Date	Hour	Summary of Events and Information	Remarks and references to Appendices
CANAL BANK WEST.	26/12/17		Work as on 25/12/17.	25/12/17
	27/12/17		Lecture 1. morning. Bumps track new work. 3 + 4 Work on improved Battery positions. 2. Work at ADMIRALS ROAD & BOUNDARY ROAD. Capt RUW regained unit - from leave.	Work.
	28/12/17		Do. Do. Do. 2/Lt. F.W. BURNETT proceeded to FLEXICOURT. for Course.	Work.
	29/12/17		Do. Do. Do.	Work.
	30/12/17		Do. Do. Do.	Work.
	31/12/17		Do. Do. Do.	Work.

1-1-1918

W.H. Tamplin
Major
O.C. 604th Fd. Coy. R.E.

Army Form C. 2118.

WAR DIARY
or
INTELLIGENCE SUMMARY.
(Erase heading not required.)

504TH FD. COY. R.E.

Vol 13

Place	Date	Hour	Summary of Events and Information	Remarks and references to Appendices
CANAL BANK WEST.	1/1/18		Sections distributed for work as follows:— Section Nº 1. Manning Dumps — Back area work. 2. Erection of Stables ADMIRALS ROAD. 3rd. Work on forward Battery positions.	2D/Lt.
"	2/1/18		Work as on the 1st inst. Capt R. ROW and 506542 Corpl SUMMERS mentioned in Despatches of 2nd. Marshall Commd. in Chief.	2D/Lt. 2D/Lt.
"	3/1/18		Work as on the 1st inst.	2D/Lt.
"	4/1/18		Do Do	2D/Lt.
"	5/1/18		Do Do	2D/Lt.
"	6/1/18		Sections distribution for work as follows. Section 1 & 2. Work on forward Battery positions 3. Erection of Stables Admirals Road. 4. Manning Dumps — Back area works.	2D/Lt.
"	7/1/18.		Work as on 6th inst. Reconnaissance by O/C of line of Corps wire	2D/Lt.

Army Form C. 2118.

WAR DIARY
INTELLIGENCE SUMMARY.
(Erase heading not required.)

500th Field Coy R.E.

Place	Date	Hour	Summary of Events and Information	Remarks and references to Appendices
CANAL BANK. WEST	8/1/18		Reconnaissance of work in hand with 6/3 204 Field Co R.E. and handing over	2Lt.
"	9/1/18		Lectures 1, 2 & 3 at work on wiring on Corps line.	2Lt. 2Lt.
			& reliever from Dumps.	
"	10/1/18		Company at work on Corps line. Wire.	2Lt.
"	11/1/18		Do	2Lt.
"	12/1/18		Do	2Lt.
"	13/1/18		Do	2Lt.
"	14/1/18		Do	2Lt.
			2. POWELL to Hospital. (Sick).	
"	15/1/18		Company at work on Corps line wire.	2Lt.
"	16/1/18		Company preparing for move to new area.	2Lt.
"	17/1/18		Company move to PROVEN. Sheet 27. E.12.d.3.q.	2Lt.
PROVEN.	18/1/18		Company resting, cleaning & refitting	2Lt.

Army Form C. 2118.

WAR DIARY
or
INTELLIGENCE SUMMARY.
(Erase heading not required.)

504th Field Coy R.E.

Place	Date	Hour	Summary of Events and Information	Remarks and references to Appendices
PROVEN.	19/7/18		Company cleaning vehicles & re-fitting. Major W.H. TAMLYN. proceeded to BLENDECQUES to attend course at R.E. School of Instruction. Commenced of Company hundred vers 6 Capt R. ROW. 2nd Lieut Treony proceeded on Service Leave to U.K.	PWR 10DY. PWR
"	20/7/18		Company preparing for move.	PWR
"	21/7/18	1:10 pm.	Company proceeded by rail to THEZY-GLIMONT.	PWR
THEZY-GLIMONT	22/7/18	11:00 am.	" arrived at "	PWR
"	23/7/18		" preparing for move. 2nd Lieut Davis in charge of advance party proceeded to ROSIERES.	PWR PWR
"	24/7/18	9:00 am.	" moved by route march to ROSIERES.	PWR
ROSIERES.	25/7/18	5:00 am.	2nd Lieut Davis in charge of advance party proceeded to ROYE.	PWR
"	"	9:30 am.	Company proceeded by route march to ROYE.	PWR
ROYE.	26/7/18	8:00 am.	2nd Lieut Davis in charge of advance party proceeded to SALENCY.	PWR
"	"	9:00 am.	Company Transport in charge of Lieut Bartlett proceeded by road to SALENCY.	PWR
"	"	10:00 am.	Dismounted personnel of Company moved by lorries to SALENCY.	PWR
SALENCY.	27/7/18	10:00 am.	Company moved by route march to BEHERICOURT. And then reported to 105th Inf Bde.	PWR
"	"	9:00 am.	Reconnaissance of R.E. Dump & Billets at PIERREMANDE by Capt. R.B.S., also conference at QUIERZY with Commandant 114th Cie du Génie.	PWR
BEHERICOURT	28/7/18	9:00 am.	Reconnaissance of billets at LES BOTTES de ROUY occupied by 114th Cie du Génie by Capt. R.B.S. Company moved by route march in charge of Lieut Bartlett to PIERREMANDE. In accordance with 90th Div Bde: Order No.17/8 dated 25/7/18	3 PWR PWR 3 PWR

Army Form C. 2118.

WAR DIARY
—or—
INTELLIGENCE SUMMARY.
(Erase heading not required.)

504th Field Coy R.E.

Place	Date	Hour	Summary of Events and Information	Remarks and references to Appendices
PIERREMANDE	29/1/8		Overhauling Coy. equipment + stores on completion of move.	PWP
"	"		Reconnaissance of Line Work with officers of 14th Cie. du Genie by Capt. Prow + Sen. Officers	PWP
"	30/1/8		Work. Section No 2. Manning R.E. Dump at PIERREMANDE + CHAUNY	PWP
"	"		" " " Pumping Plant at " + TRAAST	
"	"	7·30 pm	" " " Bridge Patrol " "	PWP
"	"	11 am	" 1–3–4. Move to forward billets at Les BUTTES des ROYE at CHAUNY.–ABLINCOURT–MANICAMP. (3 groups)	PWP
"	31/1/8	11 am	Reconnaissance of Bridges in back area by Capt. Prow.	PWP
"	"		Work. Section No 2. All as for 30th inst.	PWP
"	"		" 1–3–4. Wiring 2nd defence line.	

1–2–1918

PWPtw, Capt.
o/c 504th Fd. Coy. R.E.

Army Form C. 2118.

WAR DIARY
of
INTELLIGENCE SUMMARY.
(Erase heading not required.)

594th Field Coy RE

Place	Date	Hour	Summary of Events and Information	Remarks and references to Appendices
BUTTES DE ROUY.	25/2/18		No. 1 Section. Erecting Nissen Huts. Gas proofing dugouts.	
			2 Do. Works on Causeway for MARAIS.	10 O.R.
			3 Do. Attached Left Battalion.	
			4 Do. Work on Battle Zone. Bridge Patrols &c.	
	26/2/18		Do.	70 O.R.
	27/2/18		Do.	60 O.R.
	28/2/18		Do.	60 O.R.
			Headquarters & Nos 1, 2 & 4 Sections move to SINCENY in accordance with 174th Brigade Orders. No. BM/7/67/121 dated 27/2/18.	20 O.R.

W. Llewellyn Major.
28/2/18

Army Form C. 2118.

WAR DIARY
INTELLIGENCE SUMMARY.
(Erase heading not required.)

504th Field Coy R.E.

Place	Date	Hour	Summary of Events and Information	Remarks and references to Appendices
BUTTES DE ROUY.	17/2/18		Works as on the 16th inst.	WDH.
	18/2/18		D[itt]o.	WDH.
	19/2/18		No. 3 Section moves to AMIGNY ROUY for work with 155th Battalion. Remainder of Company same as 16th inst.	WDH.
	20/2/18		Work as on the 19th.	WDH.
	21/2/18		D[itt]o. D[itt]o.	WDH.
	22/2/18		D[itt]o. D[itt]o.	WDH.
	23/2/18		D[itt]o. D[itt]o.	WDH.
	24/2/18		No. 4 Section moves to BUTTE de ROUY. 2 " commences Work on Canvassing. 1 + 3 as on the 19th inst. Lieutenant H. G. PEARSE joined for Duty as Reinforcement.	WDH.

Army Form C. 2118.

WAR DIARY

INTELLIGENCE SUMMARY.

(Erase heading not required.)

Place	Date	Hour	Summary of Events and Information	Remarks and references to Appendices
Butte de ROUY	11/2/18		Work as on the 6th February. Reconnaissance of Battle Zone by O/C.	WXT.
	12/2/18		Work as on the 6th February.	WXT.
	13/2/18		Do.	WXT.
	14/2/18		Do. Work on Battle Zone handed over to O/C 92nd Field Coy R.E.	WXT.
	15/2/18		Work. Nos. 1 & 3 Sections work on 2nd Defence line. Wiring Manning Dump. Bridge Parties to Dugouts for Yorkville Lucerne. 2 " " 4 " "	WXT.
	16/2/18		Work. Nos. 1 & 3 Section work on 2nd Defence line. Wiring 2 " " Dugouts for Yorkville Mannery 4 " " Manning Dumps. Bridge Parties to	WXT.

WAR DIARY

INTELLIGENCE SUMMARY

Army Form C. 2118.

504TH FD. COY. R.E.

Place	Date	Hour	Summary of Events and Information	Remarks and references to Appendices
PIERREMANDE	1/1/8		**Work.** No 2 Section. Manning R.E. Dumps at PIERREMANDE & CHAUNY. Pump at PRAAST. Bridge patrol at CHAUNY. - ABLINCOURT-MANICAMP (3 groups) Nos 1-3-4 Sections. Wire entanglements on 2nd Defence Line.	P.M.R.
"		9-30am	Reconnaissance of wiring on 2nd Defence Line by Capt. Ross with C.R.E. 58th Divn. " Dug-out work at SINCENY & LAFORTELLE by Lt. Warr.	
"	2/1/8		**Work.** No 2 Section. As for 1st inst. " 1-3 " " " " " " 4. Constructing dug-outs at SINCENY & LAFORTELLE. Capt: Ross & Lt. Bartlett, laying out for work at 70 D.N.W. 120090, H.21 & H.27.	P.M.R.
"	3/1/8		**Work.** All Sections as for 2nd inst. Pump at PIERREMANDE taken over by III Corps.	P.M.R.
"		9-0am	Reconnaissance for new wire entanglement on Corps Battle Line by Capt. Ross with C.R.E. 58th Divn.	P.M.R.
"	4/1/8		**Work.** All Sections as for 3rd inst. Pump at PRAAST taken over by III Corps. Men at R.E. Dump CHAUNY released by III Corps	P.M.R.
"		4-30pm	Capt. Ross reported on 2nd Defence Line & other work in hand to Brigadier 90th Inf: Bde. P.M.R. Lt. Burnett returned from Course	
"	5/1/8		**Work.** All Sections as for 4th inst.	
"		9-30am	Reconnaissance of Corps Battle Line by Capt. Ross & Lt. Burnett.	P.M.R.
"		2 P.M.	Interview at LES BUTTES de ROUY between C.E. III Corps, O/C. & Lt. Burnett in connection with work on Corps Battle Line.	P.M.R.

Army Form C. 2118.

WAR DIARY
or
INTELLIGENCE SUMMARY.
(Erase heading not required.)

504TH FD. COY. R.E.

Place	Date	Hour	Summary of Events and Information	Remarks and references to Appendices
PIERREMANDE	5/2/18	(contd.) 4:30pm.	O/C. Lieut Burnett reported at 90th Inf. Bde.; in accordance with C.R.E.'s instructions appointment made for Lt Burnett to see Brigadier at 9.15 on 6/2/18 regarding work on Corps Battle Line.	P.P.P.
LesBUTTE de ROUY. Map ref: 20INW. H.1.c.3.2.	6/2/18		Co. H.Q. moved to advanced billets from PIERREMANDE. Work: Nos 1. & 3. Sections wiring on 2nd & Corps Battle Lines respectively. " 4 " { Dug-out work at Bn: H.Q. LaForelle, " Bde.HQ. SINCENY. " 2. Manning R.E. Dump PIERREMANDE Bridge Patrol at CHAUNY-ABLINCOURT-MANICAMP. (3 Groups)	P.P.P.
do.	7/2/18		Work: Lieut Trery returned from leave in U.K. Lieut Burnett, reconnaissance of Corps Battle Line. " Davis & Trery " " Bridges at CHAUNY. All Sections, as for 6th inst.	P.P.P.
do.	8/2/18		Work. All Sections, as for 6th inst. No 2 Sec: Repairing small Trestle Bridge in accordance III Corps Instructions G/1740/5-6/7/8 at 83.a.00. CHAUNY. Lieut Burnett, reconnaissance of Corps Battle Line with C.R.E. 58th Divn. " Davis & Trery " " Bridges at CHAUNY as on 7th inst.	P.P.P.
do.	9/2/18		Work: All Sections, as for 6th inst. Lieut Burnett, Davis & Trery.- Reconnaissances continued as on 8th inst.	P.P.P.
do.	10/2/18		Work: All Sections as for 6th inst. Major O/H Tamlyn returned from course and took over Command of Company from Capt. Potts.	P.P.P.

WAR DIARY

INTELLIGENCE SUMMARY

(Erase heading not required.)

Army Form C. 2118.

Place	Date	Hour	Summary of Events and Information	Remarks and references to Appendices
SINCENY.	1/3/18.		Sections distributed for Work as follows:-	
			No. 1 Section. Making Sanitaire Annex. Improving accommodation of new Billets	
			2 " Work on Causeway. Le MARAIS.	
			3 " Attached to 15 Hpf Battalion	WOT.
			4 " Preparing duplicate levels thro' Battle Line	
	2/3/18.		No. 1 Section. Work on Causeway. Repairing Runners.	
			2 " Work on Battle Line. Repairing Runners	
			3 " Attached Hpf Battalion	WOT.
			4 " Work on W.D.S. Sinceny. Preparing duplicate levels re	WOT.
	3/3/18.		Same as on the 2/3/18.	WOT.
	4/3/18.		Same as on the 2/3/18.	WOT.
	5/3/18.		No. 3 Section returns to Sinceny. No. 7 men at AMIGNY & 7 men at LA FORTELLE. 2-Lieut DAVIS, J.F. proceeded on leave to U.K.	
			No. 1 Section Work on Causeway	
			2 " Work on Battle Line. Gasoleinums & Butts	
			3 " Work on Battle Line. Gasoleinums & Butts	
			4 " Work in Battle Line, & Sinceny Dugouts. Bridge Demolitions.	WOT

A5834 Wt. W4973/M687 750,000 8/16 D. D. & L. Ltd. Forms/C.2118/13

Army Form C. 2118.

WAR DIARY

INTELLIGENCE SUMMARY.

(Erase heading not required.)

504TH FD. COY. R.E.

Instructions regarding War Diaries and Intelligence Summaries are contained in F. S. Regs., Part II. and the Staff Manual respectively. Title pages will be prepared in manuscript.

Place	Date	Hour	Summary of Events and Information	Remarks and references to Appendices
SINCENY	6/3/18		Work as on the 5th inst	WDH
	7/3/18		Do	WDH
	8/3/18		Do	WDH
			Lt BARTLETT returned from leave	
	9/3/18		Do	WDH
	10/3/18		Do	WDH
	11/3/18		Do	WDH
	12/3/18		Do (also party working on R.F.A. gun curtains)	WDH
	13/3/18		Do	WDH
	14/3/18		Do Reconnaissance of water supply by Lt BARTLETT	WDH
	15/3/18		Do	WDH

WAR DIARY
INTELLIGENCE SUMMARY.

Army Form C. 2118.

(Erase heading not required.)

Instructions regarding War Diaries and Intelligence Summaries are contained in F. S. Regs., Part II. and the Staff Manual respectively. Title pages will be prepared in manuscript.

Place	Date	Hour	Summary of Events and Information	Remarks and references to Appendices
SINCENY	16/3/18		Work on in the 15th inst	WDY
	17/3/18		D° D°	WDY
	18/3/18		Rehearsal of Bridge Demolitions by Section 4 Headquarters. Remainder of Section 1. Work in Sanctuaire. Section 2. Work in Battle Zone Headquarters for 291 R.F.A. Brigade. 3. Work in Battle Zone Headquarters	WDY
	19/3/18		Section 1. Work on Battle Zone Headquarters. 2. D° 3. D° 4. D° Survey Bridges, Paths, Bridge Knives & preparing Demolitions (for Bridge Firing)	WDY WDY
	20/3/18		Work as on the 19th inst.	WDY
	21/3/18	6.25 am	Orders received from Battle Station taken. Section 4 takes up position CHAUNY BRIDGES. Sections 1, 2, & 3. stand to at SINCENY.	
		9. pm	Section 2 & Supp 1 + 3 (forming 2 Sections) move to VIRY NOREUIL under Lieut PEARSE	WDY

WAR DIARY
INTELLIGENCE SUMMARY.
(Erase heading not required.)

Army Form C. 2118.

Place	Date	Hour	Summary of Events and Information	Remarks and references to Appendices
22/5/18 SINCENY	22/3/18	a.m.	As on the 21st inst. Party under Corpl. PASSMORE fixing cribs at BUTTES de ROUY. } ADT	
	23/3/18		420484 Sapper WALLACE. W. wounded. Mr BARTLETT admitted to Hospital, sick. Sections 1 & 5 learning 3 NCO dugout Battn Posts at G.14.b.central & G.10.c.5.3.} ADT	
	24	2.30	2 Sections under Lieut PEARSE return from VIRY NOREUIL.	
		9.20	Orders received from R.R.E. by O/C Demolitions, CHAUNY to destroy Bridges. Order duly carried out.	
		p.m. 3.0	Pontoon Bridge over OISE at G.4.c.9.1. destroyed.	
		7.0	2 Sections digging Platoon Posts at G.15.b.8 & G.15.a.6.2.	20 ft.
		9.0	Company moved to BIGNICOURT by orders of C.R.E. Bridge at CONDREN B.19.a.9.3. destroyed.	
PIERRE-MANDE	25.	noon 12.0	Company moved to PIERREMANDE Transport to BAC DARBLINCOURT	
		p.m. 2.0	2 Sections digging running trench on line South of AUTREVILLE running from G.23.c.9.5 & G.24.a.7.2. } 30 ft.	
		7.0	2 Sections ditto	
	26.	a.m. 7.0	3 Sections move to ABLINCOURT by orders of C.R.E. for construction of Bridge over PARTOUILLE to OISE-AISNE Canal	20 ft.

Army Form C. 2118.

WAR DIARY
INTELLIGENCE SUMMARY.
(Erase heading not required.)

Place	Date	Hour	Summary of Events and Information	Remarks and references to Appendices
PIERRE-MANDE	26/3/18		Continued 1 Section working on construction of line, south of AUTREVILLE.	ADVT
	27/3/18		Work as on 26/3/18	ADVT
	28/3/18		Sections 1 & 2 working on intermediate line south of AUTREVILLE. " 3 & 4 standing by for forming PONTOON BRIDGES over BAC D'ARBLINCOURT. Transport moved to Sheet 70 F. R. 12.a.3.3.	ADVT
	29/3/18		Work as on the 28th inst. Night of 29/30. Party building foot-bridge over St. LAZARE CANAL. G.6.b.8.7.	ADVT
	30/3/18		Work as on the 28th inst.	ADVT
	31/3/18	a.m. 7.0 10.15	Orders received from 175th Infantry Brigade to stand to at Quittle Station. Orders received to stand down. Work was on the 29th inst.	ADVT ADVT ADVT

W.T Stanhope
Major

58th Div.

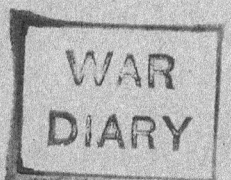

504th FIELD COMPANY, R.E.

A P R I L

1 9 1 8

Army Form C. 2118.

WAR DIARY
or
INTELLIGENCE SUMMARY.
(Erase heading not required.)

504TH FD. COY. R.E.

Vol 16

Place	Date	Hour	Summary of Events and Information	Remarks and references to Appendices
PIERRE-MANDE.	1/4/18		2 Sections work on BICHANCOURT — AUTREVILLE line. Party making height of western Bridge over St LAZARE CANAL nth of CHAUNY SUD. 2 Sections dismantling Pontoon Bridge over OISE – AISNE Canal and running same to PIERREMANDE. Letter of appreciation from Genl FERAUD commanding 1st French Cavalry Corps. Work handed over to French authorities. Company move to St AUBIN.	WDH copy heurits
	2/4/18			WDH
	3/4/18		Company moved to Quincy. South of VASSENS.	WDH
	4/4/18		Company move to CUTRY.	WDH
	5/4/18		Company move to LONGPONT for entraining. Transport entrained at 7.45 p.m.	WDH
Near CAGNY.	6/4/18		Transport detrained at LONGEAU at 6 a.m. turned to Sher. 62.D. N-31-a-1-5. 4 Sections (horsing party for Brigade) detrained at 3 p.m. turned to ditto. Wire pickets sent up to forward Dump for work next day.	WDH
	7/4/18	2 pm 7 pm	Reconnaissance of work on Reserve Defence line by O/C r8 officers. 2 Sections commence wiring line. 2 D° D°	WDH

A 5834 Wt. W4973/M687 750,000 8/16 D. D. & L. Ltd. Forms/C.2118/13

WAR DIARY

INTELLIGENCE SUMMARY

504TH FD. COY. R.E.

(Erase heading not required.)

Army Form C. 2118.

Instructions regarding War Diaries and Intelligence Summaries are contained in F.S. Regs., Part II. and the Staff Manual respectively. Title pages will be prepared in manuscript.

Place	Date	Hour	Summary of Events and Information	Remarks and references to Appendices
New CAGNY.	8/4/18		Sections working on Reserve Defence lines.	WHT.
	9/4/18		Do	WHT.
	10/4/18		Do	WHT.
	11/4/18		Do	WHT.
	12/4/18		Do	WHT.
	13/4/18		Do	WHT.
	14/4/18		Do	WHT.
	15/4/18		568 A.T. Co R.E. reported. Took over work on Right sector Reserve Defence line. Do. The undermentioned N.C.O's men received the following Awards:	WHT.

506576. Corpl. SPURLOCK. E. P. Bar to Military Medal
506480. Cpl. GILHAM. J. Military Medal
430287. L/Cpl. CROMPTON. A.E. Do
506497. Sapper RICHARDSON. W. R. Do
410255. " PATTULLO. R. Do

A5834 Wt. W4973/M687 750,000 8/16 D.D.&L. Ltd. Forms/C.2118/13

410255. Sapper PATTULLO. R. Wounded - Shell Splinter. WHT.

Instructions regarding War Diaries and Intelligence
Summaries are contained in F.S. Regs., Part II.
and the Staff Manual respectively. Title pages
will be prepared in manuscript.

WAR DIARY
INTELLIGENCE SUMMARY.

(Erase heading not required.)

504TH FD. COY. R.E.

Place	Date	Hour	Summary of Events and Information	Remarks and references to Appendices
NEUX CAGNY.	16/4/18		Sections working on Reserve Defences	
	17/4/18		Do. †Dismounting Nissen Hut at DURY.	1 Offr.
	18/4/18		Do. Erecting Nissen Hut Shelters for Bde HQ	1 Offr.
			2d Lieutenant moving forward 6 Billets T.6.d.7.5.	1 Offr.
	19/4/18		Nos. 2 & 4 Sections working on Accommodation for 2/2, 5/3, 1-3/4 Brigades	
			Nos. 3 Do. do. 173	
			No. 1. Do A Brigade HQ & A.D.S.	2 Offr.
	20/4/18		Erecting Bombproof barricade round Tents	
			Seaforth. 2nd Lieut. ↑ of Nr. 1. Section moved to Bullets T.6.d.7.5. Reinforcements.	
	21/4/18		Works on 19th inst.	2 Offr.
			Sapper GOWARD. C.	
	22/4/18		Works as on the 19th inst.	2 Offr.
			Do.	2 Offr.
	23/4/18		Do	2 Offr.
	24/4/18	a.m. 9 O. 9.30	Orders received to standby my camp.
No. 2 Lt Lieutenant ↑ refugees ↑ for prisoner Bullets to rendezvous with 8 R.E.'s orders.	2 Offr.

INTELLIGENCE SUMMARY.

504TH FD. COY. R.E.

(Erase heading not required.)

Place	Date	Hour	Summary of Events and Information	Remarks and references to Appendices
CACHY	25/4/18		Company standing by in camp. Works on camouflage screen at FORT MANOIR No 3 Sub sec.	WDT.
	26/4/18	P.M 7.30	Do.	WDT.
	~~27/4/18~~		Company employed on wiring front line in HANGARD WOOD.	WDT.
	27/4/18	a.m 11.30	Company (less Transport) moved to AMIENS and entrained for SOUES. Transport staged at COULONVILLERS.	WDT.
COULONVILLERS	28/4/18		Transport of Company arrived at COULONVILLERS.	WDT.
	29/4/18		Company cleaning Equipment &c &c.	WDT.
	30/4/18		Do.	WDT.

W.J. Crawley, Major.
O.C. 504TH FD. COY. R.E.

Copy.

58th Divn. No. A.5/10,020.
C.R.E. 58th Divn. No. A. 2922

C.R.E.

I am directed to inform you that General FERAUD, Comdg 1st French Cavalry Corps, has expressed his appreciation of the good work that has been done by the Engineers of this Division. He was especially pleased with the care that has been taken under the direction of Major BYWATER for the blowing up and destruction of bridges and for the general defensive works on the Canal.

I am to add that the G.O.C. wishes Major BYWATER and all concerned to be so informed, as he considers that great credit is due to him and all those working under him for the amount of work they have been able to carry out before & since the offensive started.

30/3/18

(SD) A. McNALTY,
Lt. Col.
A.A. & Q.M.G. 58th Division

O.C. 503rd Fld Coy R.E.
O.C. 504th Fld Coy R.E.
O.C. 511th Fld Coy R.E.

While it gives me the greatest pleasure to pass on this high appreciation by the French Corps Commander, I should like to take this opportunity of saying how proud I am of my Sappers. It is indeed a great pride & pleasure to be able to feel that I can with supreme confidence call for your loyal and zealous devotion to duty in any place and in any circumstances.

(sd) A. Savage
Lt. Col. R.E.
CRE 58th Division

30/3/18.

CONFIDENTIAL WD17

WAR DIARY
OF
504th FIELD COY. R.E.

FROM 1-5-18 TO 31-5-18

VOL. 17

Army Form C. 2118.

WAR DIARY
INTELLIGENCE SUMMARY.
(Erase heading not required.)

504th FIELD COY RE

Place	Date	Hour	Summary of Events and Information	Remarks and references to Appendices
COULON-VILLERS	1/5/18		Company Rest Training	WDT
	2/5/18		Do	WDT
	3/5/18		Do	WDT
	4/5/18		Do	WDT
	5/5/18		Do	WDT
	6/5/18		Whole Company out through Musketry practice and rifle range.	WDT
	7/5/18		Transport of Company move to Staying Green BOURDON. (173rd Inf Bde Order No 15) Remainder portion of Company move by Bus to BOIS de MOLLIENS (Bn) Transport of Company move to concentration	WDT
BAIZIEUX	8/5/18		Whole of Company move to BOIS de ROBERT, BAIZIEUX. C.R.E. Order No 19/270 dated 7.5.18	WDT
	9/5/18		Reconnaissance of Works in BAIZIEUX Béhencourt WARLOY Sector laying out new work	WDT
	10/5/18		Company working in BAIZIEUX Béhencourt WARLOY Sector	WDT

WAR DIARY

INTELLIGENCE SUMMARY.

(Erase heading not required.)

Army Form C. 2118.

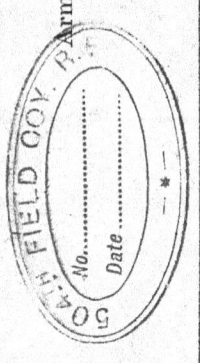
50th FIELD COY. R.E.

Place	Date	Hour	Summary of Events and Information	Remarks and references to Appendices
BAIZIEUX	11/5/18		Company working on BAIZIEUX Defences. WARLOY Sector.	W.D.T.
	12/5/18		Do.	W.D.T.
	13/5/18		Do.	W.D.T.
	14/5/18		Do.	W.D.T.
	15/5/18		Do.	W.D.T.
	16/5/18		Reconnaissance of proposed work by O/C with Officers of 520 Field Coy R.E. Work as on 10th 15th inst.	W.D.T.
VARLOY.	17/5/18		Dismounted portion of Company move to WARLOY. Taking over billets of 520 Transport of Company move to (Map Ref. 62 D.N.W) C.5.C.9.9. Billets to R.E. dis. as on W.D.T.	W.D.T.
	18/5/18		2 Sections setting out repairing & supervising digging of Trench in W.19. (Sheet 57.D.) S.E. Do.	W.D.T.
	19/5/18		2 Sections : Do. 1 Section : repairing road in V.29. (Sheet 57.D.) S.E.	W.D.T.
	20/5/18		Company working on excavation of Sidney Street C.T. waterworn Do.	W.D.T.

Army Form C. 2118.

WAR DIARY
INTELLIGENCE SUMMARY.
(Erase heading not required.)

Instructions regarding War Diaries and Intelligence Summaries are contained in F. S. Regs., Part II. and the Staff Manual respectively. Title pages will be prepared in manuscript.

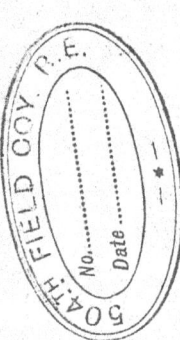
504TH FIELD COY. R.E.
No.........
Date........

Place	Date	Hour	Summary of Events and Information	Remarks and references to Appendices
WARLOY	21/5/18.		Company working on decoration of SIDNEY STREET. C.T. WARLOY BATHS &c.	WOT.
	22/5/18.		Reconnaissance of Work on front line system by Lecturer Officers. Lectures improving SIDNEY STREET. C.T. Reconnoitres at Work on WARLOY Baths, 173" Bde HdQrs &c	WOT
#	23/5/18.		Company move to forward billets. V. W. A. 6. A. 2 Lecturer atwork improving front line trench under 173" Infy Bde. to Purchase reconnaissance MELBOURNE Trench	WOT.
			1 pn purchase reconnaissance Company Billets 495.256. Sapper RHODES. G.A. Killed. 506 H 64 Sapper DODD. W. T. wounded.	
HENENCOURT WOOD.	24/5/18		Work on on the 23" inst. Extract from London Gazette. The mentioned Officer N.C.O are mentioned Despatches of Field Marshal, C in C. Lt. (Act g Major) W. H. TAMLYN. 506 H 64 Corpl. DODD. W.T. B" B"	WOT WOT
	25/5/18.			
	26/5/18.		Work carry 24" inst.	WOT

Army Form C. 2118.

WAR DIARY

INTELLIGENCE SUMMARY.

(Erase heading not required.)

Place	Date	Hour	Summary of Events and Information	Remarks and references to Appendices
HENEN-COURT WOOD	27/5/18		Work as on the 26th inst.	
	28/5/18		Do.	Do.
	29/5/18		Do.	Do.
	30/5/18		Do.	Do.
	31/5/18		Do.	Do.

W Gandyn Major
O.C. 504TH FD. Coy. R.E.
31-5-18

Vol 18

WAR DIARY
OF
504th (WESSEX) FIELD COY RE
FOR PERIOD 1-6-18 TO 30-6-18

Vol. XVII

WAR DIARY
or
INTELLIGENCE SUMMARY.

Army Form C. 2118.

(Erase heading not required.)

Place	Date	Hour	Summary of Events and Information	Remarks and references to Appendices
HEMEN-COURT WOOD.	1/9/18		Company move to BOIS de SAUVILLE. Map. 62 D.C.5.c.9.9. by our Transport.	WDT.
BOIS de SAUVILLE	2/9/18		Reconnaissance of Warloy Sector by O.C.	WDT.
	3/9/18		Work on BAISEUX System. (WARLOY Sector).	WDT.
	4/9/18		Do.	WDT.
	5/9/18		Company moves to Wood near MIRVAUX. Map. 57.a. T.26.a.9.9.	WDT.
MIRVAUX	6/9/18		Company erecting Camp & overhauling vehicles.	WDT.
	7/9/18		Company training as per programme rendered to C.R.E.	WDT.
	8/9/18		Do	WDT.
	9/9/18		Church Parade with 173rd Infy Bde and Inspection by Same. III Corps	WDT.

Army Form C. 2118.

WAR DIARY
or
INTELLIGENCE SUMMARY.

(Erase heading not required.)

Instructions regarding War Diaries and Intelligence Summaries are contained in F. S. Regs., Part II. and the Staff Manual respectively. Title pages will be prepared in manuscript.

Place	Date	Hour	Summary of Events and Information	Remarks and references to Appendices
MIRVAUX	10/6/18		Company move to SAVEUSE. Dismounted Personnel by Motor Lorry, Mounted Personnel by road.	WdT
SAVEUSE	11/6/18		Company Training. Water Reconnaissance.	WdT.
	12/6/18		Do. Water Reconnaissance of 173rd Bde Area.	WdT.
	13/6/18		Do.	WdT.
	14/6/18		Do.	WdT
	15/6/18.		Do.	WdT.
	16/6/18.		Do.	WdT
BOIS DE MOLLIENS	17/6/18.		Company move to BOIS DE MOLLIENS. Dismounted Personnel by 'Bus Transport by road.	WdT.
BOIS ROBERT	18/6/18.		Company move to BOIS DE ROBERT.	WdT
LAVIEVILLE	19/6/18.		Reconnaissance of line by O/c Section Officers & 2 Sections move on to forward billets.	WdT.

WAR DIARY
or
INTELLIGENCE SUMMARY.

(Erase heading not required.)

Army Form C. 2118.

Place	Date	Hour	Summary of Events and Information	Remarks and references to Appendices
LAVIEVILLE	20/6/18		2 Sections working on front line system 173rd Brigade sector.	Unit.
	21/6/18		Do	Unit.
	22/6/18		Do	Unit.
	23/6/18		Do	Unit.
	24/6/18		Do	Unit.
	25/6/18		Do	Unit.
			Headquarters move to BOIS DE ROBERT.	
BOIS de ROBERT	26/6/18		Do	Unit.
	27/6/18		Major W.H. Tomalyn proceeds on leave to U.K. Capt R Row taken over command of Company	Unit.

Army Form C. 2118.

WAR DIARY
or
INTELLIGENCE SUMMARY.
(Erase heading not required.)

Instructions regarding War Diaries and Intelligence Summaries are contained in F. S. Regs., Part II. and the Staff Manual respectively. Title pages will be prepared in manuscript.

Place	Date	Hour	Summary of Events and Information	Remarks and references to Appendices
BOIS de ROBERT	28/8		2 Sections working on Front line System 173 Infy. Brigade Sector.	PMP PMP
"			Transport Lines moved to C.5.a.8.7 Sheet 62D N.W. 20000 Co.H.Q. & details	
BAIZIEUX	29/8		2 Sections working on Front line System 173 Infy Brigade Sector	PMP PMP
"	30/8		2 " " " " " " "	PMP PMP

O.C. 504TH FD. COY. R.E.
30/6/18

Y/8/19

War Diary
of
504th (Wessex) Field Co. R.E.
for Period
1-7-18 to 31-7-18

VOL. XVIII

Army Form C. 2118.

WAR DIARY
INTELLIGENCE SUMMARY
(Erase heading not required.)

504TH FIELD COY. R.E.

Place	Date	Hour	Summary of Events and Information	Remarks and references to Appendices
BAIZIEUX	1/8		2 Sections working on Front line System with 173 Inf: Bde: Sector.	PMB
do.	2/8		2 " " " " Co.H.Q. Accommodation Hutse lines	
do.	2/8		Capt: H.L. Pugsley RE reported for attachment to Co for one months tour of duty	PMB
			Lt: F.D. Edwardes & 7 Sergts: of 114th Suffolk Pioneers reported for two weeks attachment for R.E. training.	
do.	3/8		Reconnaissance of Reserve Brigade Area by Capt: Prov with O.C. 511 Fld: CoRE prior to relief on night of 2-3/8 in accordance with C.R.E's O.O. No.53 dated 29/8.	PMB
			2 Sections move from forward billets to Co.H.Q.	
do.	4/8		3 Sections on works in Reserve Brigade Area.	
			1 " " erecting Divisional Baths at MIRVAUX	
do.	4/8		4 " " as on 3rd inst.	PMB
do.	5/8		4 " " ditto	
do.	6/8		Reconnaissance of Reserve Brigade Area by O.C. 503 Fld. CoRE and Capt Prov.	PMB
			" " Left Brigade Area by Section officers prior to relieving 503 Fld CoR.E on night of 6-7/8 in accordance with C.R.E's O.O. No.54 dated 5/8	PMB
do.	6/8	7.30 pm	3 Sections moved to forward billets at D.19.a.5.0. Co.H.Q. remaining at C.5.a.8.7.	PMB
do.	7/8		3 Sections on Front line works with 173rd Inf: Bde:	
			1 (No.1) in reserve at Co.H.Q. and erecting Divisional Baths at MIRVAUX.	PMB

Army Form C. 2118.

WAR DIARY
or
INTELLIGENCE SUMMARY.
(Erase heading not required.)

504th FIELD Coy. R.E.

Place	Date	Hour	Summary of Events and Information	Remarks and references to Appendices
BAIZIEUX	8/7/18		Do on 7th inst.	PMP
do	9/7/18		3 Sections (Nos 2.3.4) on front line works as for 7th inst.	PMP
			" (No 1) Completing Divisional Baths at MIRVAUX.	
			Camp Services &c at Co. H.Q.	
do	10/7/18		3 Sections (No. 2.3.4) as for 9th inst.	PMP
			1 " (No. 1) Improving Camp + extending accommodation at Co. H.Q.	
do	11/7/18		3 Sections (Nos 1.3.4) Do for 10th inst.	PMP
			No. 1 " relieved No. 2 Section at forward billets.	
			No. 2 " moved to Transport lines in place of No. 1 Sec.	
			Co. H.Q. moved to forward billets D.19.a 5.0.	
LAWRENCE WOOD D.19.a.5.0	12/7/18		3 Sections (No. 1.3.4) as for 11th inst.	PMP
			1 " (No. 2) camp accommodation at Transport lines and making Pioneer Stores	
do	13/7/18		do also as for 12th inst.	PMP
			Lt. BURNETT and 4.O.R. commenced a 6 day Instructional Course in Elementary Field Works for 173 Inf. Bde. Battle Surplus at MIRVAUX.	PMP
do	14/7/18		All as for 13th inst.	PMP
do	15/7/18		Work " " " 17th " Lieut. ARMSTRONG + 7 Sergts 8th/4 Suffolk Regt Pioneers reported	PMP
do	16/7/18		Work all " " " 15th " for 2 weeks attachment; vice 11th/F.D. Edmondes + 75 atts	PMP
			Major N.H. HAZLITT returned from Leave to U.K. resumed Command of Unit.	PMP

A577 Wt. W9791/1773 500,000 4/15 D.D. & L. A.D.S.S./Forms/C. 2118.

Army Form C. 2118.

WAR DIARY
or
INTELLIGENCE SUMMARY.
(Erase heading not required.)

504th FIELD COY RE

Place	Date	Hour	Summary of Events and Information	Remarks and references to Appendices
LAWRENCE WOOD. D.19.a.50	17/7/18		Work as on the 16th inst. 1 Lt TRERY and 2 other ranks proceeded to IV Army Rest Camp	WDH
	16/7/18		Work as on the 17th inst. Company relieved by 511th Field Co. R.E. moves to Transport lines	WDH
BAISEUX C.5.a.8.4	19/7/18		No 1. Section. Work on LAVIEVILLE LINE + Horse Shelters	
			2 ,, ,, Work on DARWIN TRENCH ditto	
			3 ,, ,, Work on BAISEUX BATHS – BAISEUX System	
			4 ,, ,, Work on Railway line BEHENCOURT.	WDH
			Lt PEARCE proceeds on leave to U.K.	
			Capt HEINZE U.S.A Engineers + 14. O.R. attached to Unit for 7 days tour of duty	WDH
	20/7/18		Work as on the 19th.	WDH
	21/7/18		Do	WDH
	22/7/18		Do	WDH
	23/7/18		Do	WDH

Army Form C. 2118.

WAR DIARY
INTELLIGENCE SUMMARY.
(Erase heading not required.)

504th FIELD COY. R.E.

Place	Date	Hour	Summary of Events and Information	Remarks and references to Appendices
BASIEUX. C.5.a.8.4.	24/7/18		Work as on the 19th inst.	WDK.T
	25/7/18		D°.	WDK.T
	26/7/18		D°.	WDK.T
			Capt HEINZE. U.S.A. Engineers & 6 other ranks returned to their unit on completion of tour of duty.	
			Lieut WINSLOW. U.S.A. Engineers & 6 other ranks attached to Unit for 7 days tour of duty.	WDK.T
	27/7/18		Work as on the 19th inst. N°2 Section constructing Bde HQrs Q150. D.26.b.9.4.	WDK.T
	28/7/18		Lt TRERY. N.H. returned to duty from V ARMY Rest Camp. Work on BAVLINCOURT Siding and LAVIEVILLE LINE handed over to 503 F.C.	WDK.T
			Sections 1, 2 & 3 Forming Company Headquarters move to Lomenne Billets. D.26.b.1.9. Lt ARMSTRONG & 4 N.C.O. 1/+ Suffolks Regt returned to Unit	WDK.T
RIBEMONT D.26.b.1.9	29/7/18		Section 1. Bridge guard. 2. Constructing Bde HQrs 3. Constructing Breastworks 4. Revetting Horse Lines at Rear Company Headquarters.	WDK.T

Army Form C. 2118.

WAR DIARY
~~INTELLIGENCE SUMMARY.~~
(Erase heading not required.)

504th FIELD COY. R.E.

Place	Date	Hour	Summary of Events and Information	Remarks and references to Appendices
RIBEMONT. D.26.b.1.9.	29/7/16		W/L CLEMENTS. E. & 4 N.C.O.s from 1/1 Battn Suffolk Regiment attached for training. Work as on the 29th inst.	WDT
	30/7/16		L. Corpl HOWE wounded. Shell splinters (at duty) No. 1 Section work on Tunnelling	WDT.
	31/7/16		Work as on the 30th inst. Bayour BUIRE.	WDT.

W. Llewelyn
Major.
O.C. 504TH FD. COY. R.E.

58th Divl. Engineers

504th FIELD COMPANY,

ROYAL ENGINEERS,

AUGUST 1918

Army Form C. 2118.

WAR DIARY
INTELLIGENCE SUMMARY.
(Erase heading not required.)

504th FIELD COY. R.E.

Place	Date	Hour	Summary of Events and Information	Remarks and references to Appendices
RIBEMONT. D.26.b.1.9	1/8/18		Work as on the 31/7/18. Sections 1. Bridge Reports – BUIRE Dugouts 2. Bridge VHQ Rd 3. Brickworks TREUX – BUIRE & Forestry Woodlanes	
	2/8/18		Do. after which Sections 1, 2 & 3 move to Transport Lines. O.S.O.B.H. on relief by 70th Field R.E.	
BAIZIEUX	3/8/18	a.m. 1.	Company (less Transport) embus expressed to BERTEAUCOURT. Transport proceeds by march route, arriving 11 a.m.	ADT.
BERTEAU-COURT.	4/8/18.	P.m. 9.30	Company (less Transport) embus expressed to BOIS de ESCARDONN-EUSE. Transport proceeds by march route. Captain ROW. R. proceeds on leave to United Kingdom	WDT. WDT.
BOIS de ESCARD-ONNEUSE. 62.D.N.W. I.15.a.9.4.	5/8/18.	a.m. 9.0	Company arrives. Existing children accommodation in Wood.	WDT.
	6/8/18		Nos. 1 & 3 Sections. Camp Improvements. 2 & 4 " Work on Road Improvement. Lieut PEARSE. H.C. returns from leave. 11 hour SPAIN. F.L. proceeds to ROUEN. R.E. Training School for Course of Instruction.	WDT. WDT. WDT.

Lieut PEARSE. H.C. returns from leave.
A.D.S.S./Forms/C. 2118.

Army Form C. 2118.

WAR DIARY

INTELLIGENCE SUMMARY

504th FIELD COY RE

(Erase heading not required.)

Instructions regarding War Diaries and Intelligence Summaries are contained in F. S. Regs., Part II. and the Staff Manual respectively. Title pages will be prepared in manuscript.

Place	Date	Hour	Summary of Events and Information	Remarks and references to Appendices
BOIS de ESCARD-ONNEUSE. J.15.a.9.6	7/8/18.		Work as on the 6th inst. Lt BURNETT attached as Liaison Officer to 173" Brigade.	WDH
	8/8/18.		Section 2. Work as usual. SAILLY LE SEC. J.29.a.6.1 to J.23.d.5.5. Remainder of Company standing by.	WDH
	9/8/18.		Section 1. Move to BIVOUAC on J.36.2.A.5. Work on 173 Bde H.Q. " 2. ,, Move to assembly position in K.31.a + Reconnoitred new front line reconnaissance route in K.17.c. returning via K.31.a. Lieut BURNETT. F.W. & Nº8386 Sapper SKINNER. wounded. gunshot wounds.	WDH
	10/8/18.		Section 2. H.Q. return to BOIS de ESCARDONNEUSE. J.15.a.9.6. 3. Revetting shuredump " 1. Continuation of work on Brigade HQ. afterwards returning to J.15.a.9.6. work in running front line in K.12. Brer. sent	WDH
	11/8/18		Section 1. 2 tps move to J.36.2.A.5. 3. Revetting Ahaux dump "	WDH
	12/8/18.		Sections 1. 2 tps move to CEMETERY COPSE. J.24 to 5-7 over or night proceeded to work in running new front line in K.12. b tree.	WDH
	13/8/18.		Sections 1. 2 tps return to BOIS de ESCARDONNEUSE. J.15.a.9.6. 3. Cleaning vehicles.	WDH

1577 Wt.W10791/1773 500,000 1/15 D. D. & L. A.D.S.S./Forms/C. 2118.

Army Form C. 2118.

WAR DIARY

~~INTELLIGENCE~~ SUMMARY.

(Erase heading not required.)

Instructions regarding War Diaries and Intelligence Summaries are contained in F. S. Regs., Part II. and the Staff Manual respectively. Title pages will be prepared in manuscript.

504th FIELD COY R.E.

Place	Date	Hour	Summary of Events and Information	Remarks and references to Appendices
BOIS DE ESCARDONN-EUSE. T.15.a.9.6. (?)	14/8/18		Company rested Brother.	W.D.T.
	15/8/18		Company Training. Lt PEARSE. H.C. acting Adjutant- 58 Divl R.E.	W.D.T.
	16/8/18		2/Lieut PRIDE. F. reported as a reinforcement	W.D.T.
	17/8/18		Company Training	W.D.T.
	18/8/18		Do	W.D.T.
	19/8/18		2/Lt DAVIS. J.F. to C.B.S. for dental treatment	W.D.T.
	20/8/18		Company Athletic Sports.	W.D.T.
	21/8/18		Company Training. Capt. R. ROW. returns from leave to U.K.	W.D.T.
	22/8/18		Company Training Lt TRERY. R. proceeded on leave to U.K.	W.D.T.
	23/8/18		Company Training	W.D.T.
	24/8/18	6.0 a.m. 4.0	Company moved to HEILLY. Company less Transport- move to K.14.d.3.4.	W.D.T.

Army Form C. 2118.

WAR DIARY

INTELLIGENCE SUMMARY.

(Erase heading not required.)

504th FIELD Coy R.E.

Instructions regarding War Diaries and Intelligence Summaries are contained in F. S. Regs., Part II. and the Staff Manual respectively. Title pages will be prepared in manuscript.

Place	Date	Hour	Summary of Events and Information	Remarks and references to Appendices
S. of MORLAN-COURT. K.14.d.3.4.	25/8/18.		"II Lt PRIDE" Section 3. attached to 173rd Brigade. Searching for Booby Traps Hawk Manor. Sections 2 & 4 & 4 platoons 1/1 Suffolk Pioneers working on forward Tracks. in F.20.26 & 27. Transport moved to K.14.d.3.4.	W.D.T.
	26/8/18.		Company (less Transport) moved to K.12.b.4.6. Transport moved to K.23.a.3.8. Section 3. attached to 173 Bde wo on the 25th " 2 M & 2 Platoons 1/1 Suffolk Pioneers working on Tracks in F.22.23 & 27 II Lt DAVIS. reported from E.O.S.	W.D.T.
GAS VALLEY K.12.b.4.6.	27/8/18.		Section 3. attached to 173 Bde wo on the 26th & 2 M & 2 Platoons 1/1 Suffolk Pioneers working on Tracks in F.21.27.28 & 29.	W.D.T.
S. of CITADEL F.21.a.7.0.	28/8/18.		Company (less Transport) move to F.21.a.7.0. Lieut PRIDE Section 3. withdrawn 173 Inft Bde. Sect. 3. working under 503 Field RE on D.H.Q. at L.1. & 3.0 " 1. H. working on mould tracks in F.22.29 & 30 & A.19.	W.D.T.

Army Form C. 2118.

WAR DIARY

INTELLIGENCE SUMMARY

504th FIELD COY. R.E

(Erase heading not required.)

Instructions regarding War Diaries and Intelligence Summaries are contained in F.S. Regs., Part II. and the Staff Manual respectively. Title pages will be prepared in manuscript.

Place	Date	Hour	Summary of Events and Information	Remarks and references to Appendices
S. of Citadel F.21.d.7.0	29/8/18		Section 3. Working on D.H.Q at L.1.t.3.0 Remainder of Company working on route Markers. Company moved to BILLON WOOD VALLEY. A.25.d.6.7.	WDT
BILLON WOOD VALLEY	30/8/18		No. 1. Section. attached to 173 Brigade. Standing by. 2 & 3 " Work on new D.H.Q at A.19.t.5.1. 4 " " Work on Roads nr A.30 & B.14.	WDT
	31/8/18		No. 1 Section. attached to 173 Brigade. Standing by 2 & 3. Work on Route-Tracelle Wells 4. Work on Transport Lines. Clearing roads in Billon Wood Valley	WDT

W.R.Gawdyn
Major.
O.C. 504TH FD. COY. R.E.

1-9-1918

WAR DIARY

of

504th (WESSEX) FIELD Coy R.E.(T)

For Period

1-9-18 to 30-9-18

Vol. XIX.

Army Form C. 2118.

WAR DIARY
INTELLIGENCE SUMMARY.
504TH FIELD COY. R.E.

(Erase heading not required.)

Place	Date	Hour	Summary of Events and Information	Remarks and references to Appendices
BILLON WOOD VALLEY A.25.d.6.7.	1/9/18.		No. 1 Section attached to 173 Bde. Improving accommodation for Pers B.23.c	
			3 " " Work on Trestle Roads	
			2 " " loading pontoons at BRICKYARD. K.16.c transporting to CARNOY.	WDT
	2/9/18.		Company relieved by 439 Zealand Co. R.E.	
			Nos. 1 & 2 Sections. Work on Bde H.Q. B.23.c	WDT
			3 " Collecting Salvage	
	3/9/18.		Nos. 1 & 2 Sections. Work on Bde H.Q. B.23.c	WDT
			3 " Work on D.H.Q. MAUREPAS	
	4/9/18.		Company move to (62.c.N.W) B.22.c.3.7. N of HEM.	WDT
N of HEM	5/9/18.		Company resting reconstructing Billets	WDT
	6/9/18.		Company moved to BOUCHESVESNES. Pontoons fetched from CARNOY & parked at R.E. Dump. BOUCHESVESNES. cont.	
BOUCHESVESNES	7/9/18		Company moved to C.24.a.8.1. MOISLAINS. Reconnaissance for Pioneers Trestle Station. Capt. It. L. BAZALGETTE proceeds to 511 Field Co R.E.	WDT
MOISLAINS				

Army Form C. 2118.

WAR DIARY
INTELLIGENCE SUMMARY.
504TH FIELD COY. R.E.
(Erase heading not required.)

Place	Date	Hour	Summary of Events and Information	Remarks and references to Appendices
MOISLAINS.	8/9/18.		No 4. Section attached to 173 Bde.	
			1. " working from NURLU to LIERMONT.	
			2. " " WATER-PUMPING STATION. LIERAMONT.	WDG
	9/9/18.		ii Lt TRERY. N.H. rejoined from leave to U.K.	
			No 4. Section attached to 173 Bde	
			1. " work on trestles.	WDG.
	10/9/18.		2 & 3. " work on Pumping Station, LIERAMONT.	
			Military Medals awarded to the following :-	
			506052. Cpl. DAY. E.C.	
			505481. 2nd Cpl. LATCHAM. A.E	
			506055. L Cpl. WHITE. S.J.	WDG
	11/9/18.		Work as on the 10th inst.	WDG
	12/9/18.		Work as on the 10th inst.	
			Company with Transport move to D.5.d.3.0. (Map. 62 C.N.E).	WDG.

Army Form C. 2118.

504TH FIELD COY. R.E.

WAR DIARY
INTELLIGENCE SUMMARY.
(Erase heading not required.)

Instructions regarding War Diaries and Intelligence Summaries are contained in F.S. Regs, Part II. and the Staff Manual respectively. Title pages will be prepared in manuscript.

Place	Date	Hour	Summary of Events and Information	Remarks and references to Appendices
S.E. of NURLU.	13/9/18		Work as on the 10th inst.	WDT
	14/9/18		Do. Do. Capt R. ROW proceeded to FORGES LES EAUX to attend Class of Instruction in Stores Management.	WDT
	15/9/18		Do. Do. Camp bombed by E.A. 2/Lieut SPAIN F.L. rejoined unit from Engineering Course.	WDT WDT RZP
	16/9/18		Do. Do. 2/Lieut SPAIN F.L. the animals killed on rouen.	WDT RZP
	17/9/18		Work as on the 10th inst.	RZP
	18/9/18		Do.	
	19/9/18		Do. 1 Section under 2/Lt Davis engaged in spout drill with 173rd Inf Brigade. 2/Lt Pute and 12 men reconnoitering sector Major W.H. TAMLYN wounded and evacuated to C.C.S. Capt. ORUM F.C. wounded and evacuated to C.C.S. 2/Lieut H.G. PEARSE No. 506567 Sapper ORUM F.C. 58 Div. and took over command of unit rejoined unit from C.R.E. 58 Div. No 2 Section work on water points at No. 4 Section attached to 173 Inf Brigade. Nos 1 and 3 Sections standing by for orders LIERAMONT.	RZP RZP
	20/9/18		No. 4 Section attached 173 Inf Bde. Nos 1 & 3 Sections work on overland tracks	RZP
	21/9/18		No 4 Section returned from attachment to 173 Inf Bde. Nos 1 & 3 Sections as on 20th No. 2 Section as on. Antrivous Batts NURLU.	RZP
	22/9/18			RZP

C.H. Som 21-9-18

Army Form C. 2118.

WAR DIARY
INTELLIGENCE SUMMARY.
(Erase heading not required.)

504TH FIELD COY. R.E.

Place	Date	Hour	Summary of Events and Information	Remarks and references to Appendices
S.E. of NURLU	23/6		Capt R. ROW returns from Course and takes over command of Company	PRB
			1 Section work on Bath House NURLU	
	24/6		2 " " " overland Track.	PRB
			1 " " " revetting horse lines at Co. Billets.	
	25/6		Co. moves to MONTAUBAN. (57.c.5.21.&1.6.)	PRB
MONTAUBAN.			Dismounted by Bus Convoy with 113 Inf. Bde.	PRB
			Transport " route march " "	
	26/6		Co. cleaning vehicles preparing for move.	
	27/6	8am	Co. moved by route march to Rail-head MERICOURT & entrains with 113 Inf.Bde.Coys.	PRB
		7.55am	Co. detrains at ACQ. (LENS.11. Map) & proceeds by route march to LAPENDU Camp.	PRB
LAPENDU.	28/6		Co. cleans vehicles & stands by for move.	
			Capt ROW & Lt. N.H. TRERY proceed to BULLY GRENAY to take over work in this Area.	PRB
			103 FIELD COY. R.E.	
	29/6	8 am.	Co. moves by route march to new H.Q. BULLY GRENAY. (R.11.c.10.15.55 Map 44.B)	PRB
			3 Sections move to forward billets in CITE ST PIERRE. (M.11.c 55.05 Map 44.B)	
BULLY GRENAY.	30/6		Reconnaissance of work in line by Section Officers, 3 Sections work on forward billets,	PRB
			1 Section clearing vehicles & taking over Divisional R.E. Dump.	

PW Row, Capt:

WAR DIARY
of
504TH FIELD Coy RE
FOR PERIOD
1-10-18 TO 31-10-18

VOL XXII

WAR DIARY

504TH FD. COY. R.E.

Army Form C. 2118.

Instructions regarding War Diaries and Intelligence Summaries are contained in F.S. Regs., Part II. and the Staff Manual respectively. Title pages will be prepared in manuscript.

(Erase heading not required.)

Place	Date	Hour	Summary of Events and Information	Remarks and references to Appendices
BULLY GRENAY	1/10		1 Section Clearing Vehicle training Riv: Dumps.	3 P.R.
			1 " work at 173 Inf: Bde: H.Q.	
			2 " " counter patrols in ST. PIERRE	
			" " " road MAROC to ST PIERRE and making "Right overland Track."	
dt.	2/10		Co. H.Q. moved to ST. PIERRE.	
			1 Section Searching Dug-outs in 173 Inf: Bde: Area.	
			1 " " on ST PIERRE Road.	
			1 " " on "RIGHT TRACK."	
			1 " " repairs to buildings at Div: H.Q.	
			Appointment.	G.R.E.
			Temp. (A/Capt.) T. ROY is appointed to Command 507th Field C.R.E. and to be Acting Major 23-9-18 since Lieut. (A/Major) W.A. Tamlyn wounded.	
			(Authority:- A.G1 No A.G. 55/7883 (0)-21-9-18)	
			C.R.E. 58th Divn. No E.13299.	
			Lieut: F.C.B. Wills. M.C. R.E.(T) reported as reinforcement from R.E. Base depôt.	
ST. PIERRE.	3/10		2/Lieut: T. Pride and 1 Section attached for duty to 173 Inf: Bde.	P.R.
			1 Section on repairs to buildings at Div: H.Q.	
			2 " " on "Right Track."	
	4/10		Co for 3-10-18.	
	5/10		As for 4-10-18.	
			Lieut. F.C.B. Wills. M.C. R.E.(T.) to posted to 511 Field C.R.E. (Authority R.O. No 68 dated 4/10 by C.R.E. 58th Divn.	
			No 504 A 2. W/2 Lieut: RICHARDS, T. killed by Shell at M.T.A. N.13 C.3.6.	

Army Form C. 2118.

WAR DIARY

INTELLIGENCE SUMMARY.

(Erase heading not required.)

504TH FD. COY. R.E.

Place	Date	Hour	Summary of Events and Information	Remarks and references to Appendices
ST. PIERRE.	6/10/18		No. 4 Section moved to C.H.Q. ST. PIERRE from Transport lines TULLY GRENAY.	DMP
			1 " on repairs to GT. PETER ST.	
			2 " on making "RIGHT TRACK"	
do.	7/18		attached 173 Inf. Bde." making gas curtains former track.	DMP
			2 " on "RIGHT TRACK" completed to CARVIN Road.	
			1 " on repairs to GT. PETER ST.	
			1 " attached 173 Inf. Bde. making gas curtains in forward dug-outs.	
			Reconnaissance of Railway Siding Carried out at N.11.a.3.8. (Map 744.SW2.10000) by Mr TDW and A Neill. F. PRUE.	
do	8/10/18		All four Sections do. do. 7/18	DMP
			Lt. Pride to Sappers clearing Tank mine-field in LOISON Station Yard. N.11.C.	
			1 Sec: on repairs to GT. PETER ST.	
			3 " on works in Brigade forward Area; anti-gas curtains, in CONDE station	
do	9/10/18		fly cuttings, excavating for new advanced Bde: H.Q. in LOISON STATION siding.	DMP
do	10/10/18		All four sections as for 9/18	DMP
do	11/10/18		Ditto	DMP
do	12/10/18		½ Section excavating + erecting new advanced Bde H.Q. Shutter in LOISON fly cutting.	DMP
			½ " fixing anti-gas curtains to dug-outs in Bde: area.	
			1 " repairing LENS-SALLAUMINES Rd., reconnoitering LENS, LOISON, HARNES Roads	
do	13/10/18		1 " erecting Anti-gas curtains,	DMP
			1 " repairing, LENS-HARNES Road.	
			2 " Adv: Bde: H.Q. in LOISON fly Cutting,	

WAR DIARY

INTELLIGENCE SUMMARY

Army Form C. 2118.

504TH FD. COY. R.E.

(Erase heading not required.)

Instructions regarding War Diaries and Intelligence Summaries are contained in F.S. Regs., Part II. and the Staff Manual respectively. Title pages will be prepared in manuscript.

Place	Date	Hour	Summary of Events and Information	Remarks and references to Appendices
ST. PIERRE	14/8/18		Work on Adv: Bde H.Q. LOISON Station Cutting, Auti: gas curtain in Bde: Area, repairing LENS-LOISON-HARNES Road.	PHF
HARNES.	15/8/18		Co. moves to HARNES. Transport " " LOISON.	PHF
			2nd Lieut: PRIDE & 2 Section repairing raft bridge across LAHAUTE DEULE Canal at I.29.a.7.2. & Constructing 2 foot Bridges at I.29.6.2.2 + I.29.6.5.2. ½ Section on Water & well reconnaissance in HARNES + COURRIERES 1 " " " removing obstructions in roads in COURRIERES 2 " " " Constructing heavy bridge over Canal at HARNES. O.3.d.2.0. Capt: H.L. BAZALGETTE joined Unit as 2nd in Command in accordance with CRE's 58th Divn R.O. No 67. dated 2/8	PHF
do.	16/8/18		3 Sections Constructing heavy bridge at O.3.d.2.0. 1 " " " " " " " " " 2nd Lieut: T.L. SPAIN proceeded on Service Leave to U.K. 7 Sections work as on 15/8	PHF
do.	17/8/18			PHF
do.	18/8/18		Co. H.Q. & Transport moves to COURRIERES. 7 Sections Constructing heavy bridge at P.2.a.10.25.	PHF
COURRIERES	19/8/18		Whole Co. moves to SEC MONT.	PHF
SEC MONT	20/8/18		" LAN HAY with 113 Inf: Bde: Group.	PHF

Army Form C. 2118.

WAR DIARY

INTELLIGENCE SUMMARY.

504TH FD. COY. R.E.

(Erase heading not required.)

Place	Date	Hour	Summary of Events and Information	Remarks and references to Appendices
LANNAY	20/10/18		1 Sec: attached to 1/13 Inf: Bde: for advance Guard work, forming road diversions at PLANARD. H.6. & 3.8	PRP
	21/10/18		1 Sec: Building at T.33O. d.0.0.3. under Lt: Pearce, " Building at T.33O. d.0.0.3. " " boring with hydraulic Jacks under Lt: Theny. Coy. moves with 1/13 Inf: Bde; to load pontoons for 1/13 Inf: Bde: at BERSEE Staging at BERSEE. 1 Sec: under Lt: Bride going with advance guard & forming road diversions at I.3. a.1.6. & 13. a.1.6. Filling in Craters at 13.6.7.8. & Clearing Trees. 1 Sec: Building Craters at 12.6.2.6. & billeting the night at HOWARDRIES under Lt. Pearce 1 " Completing bridge at T.3Od.03. under Lt: Theny. 1 " with bridging equipment proceeds from BERSEE to RUMEGIES under Capt Bazalgette, afterwards joining Coy at RONGY & forming barrel-pier bridge at ESPAIN. D.25. 6.8.8. for Inf: in file under Lt: Bride	PRP PRP PRP
RONGY.	22/10/18		Coy. Transport moves back to CUL DO FOUR. 1 Sec: under Lieut: H.G. Pearce joins G.H.Q. at RONGY on completion of road bridge at HOWARDRIES Pontoons of 3 Field Coy. 58th Divl: R.E. brought to RONGY WOOD under Capt Bazalgette. 3 Sec: reconnaissance for & collecting timber in BLEHARIES, Reconnaissance of river at ESPAIN by O.C. 1 Sec: making 2-100' barrel-pier foot Bridges at BLEHARIES + dumping same at Br: H.Q. ready for launching.	PRP
	23/10/18		1 Sec: materials for cribs in RONGY Wood 2 Sec: collecting Timber in BLEHARIES.	PRP

Army Form C. 2118.

WAR DIARY
INTELLIGENCE SUMMARY.
(Erase heading not required.)

504TH FD. COY. R.E.

Instructions regarding War Diaries and Intelligence Summaries are contained in F.S. Regs., Part II. and the Staff Manual respectively. Title pages will be prepared in manuscript.

Place	Date	Hour	Summary of Events and Information	Remarks and references to Appendices
RONGY	24/10/18		1 Sec: Collecting timber in BLEHARIES. 3 " making fascines in RONGY Wood. Reconnaissance of river crossing at ESPAIN by O.C.	RE
"	25/10/18		1 Sec: making fascines in RONGY Wood. 1 " cutting trees + carrying to dump in BLEHARIES. 1 " Standing by. 1 " Attempting to launch 2-100' barrel-pier foot bridges at ESPAIN at night under Lieut H.G. Pearce. Continued hostile fire prevented this being done.	RE
"	26/10/18		1 Sec: endeavouring to float + barrel rafts under O.C. + Lieut F. Poole. 2 floated when hostile fire prevented operation continuing. 1 Sec: making 5 more barrel rafts at Bn: H.Q. BLEHARIES. 1 " Standing by for pontooning. 1 " Endeavouring to launch 5 rafts at ESPAIN at night under Lieut. N. Treaybut were driven off the river bank by continued hostile shelling. Reconnaissance of river crossing by O.C.	RE
"	27/10/18		1 Sec: making 4 barrel rafts at Bn: H.Q. BLEHARIES ready for use. 1 " Collecting timber + felling trees for bridging purposes + forming dump at BLEHARIES. Remaining 2 Sec: Standing by for bridging. Reconnaissance by O.C. of Northern sector of river in Left Bde: Area.	RE
"	28/10/18		Half Co. Standing-by for bridging. 1 Sec: making barrel-pier bridge for Pack Mules at Bn: H.Q. BLEHARIES ready for use. 1 " Collecting + classifying timber to dump.	RE

Army Form C. 2118.

WAR DIARY

INTELLIGENCE SUMMARY.

(Erase heading not required.)

504TH FD. COY. R.E.

Instructions regarding War Diaries and Intelligence Summaries are contained in F. S. Regs., Part II. and the Staff Manual respectively. Title pages will be prepared in manuscript.

Place	Date	Hour	Summary of Events and Information	Remarks and references to Appendices
RONGY.	29/10/18		Half Coy. Standing-by for Bridging. 2 Sections collecting timber in BLEHARIES, making side screens & handwood for bridge. Making Barrel Pier Bridge for Pack Mules, ready for launching at BLEHARIES	PME
Do.	30/10/18		Do for 29-10-18	PME
Do.	31/10/18		Co Standing-by for Bridging. Improving Barrel Pier Bridge parts at BLEHARIES.	PME

Ph Potts Mjr.
O.C. 504TH FD. COY. R.E.

WAR DIARY

of

504th Field Company R.E.

for the period

1.11.18. to 30.11.18.

WAR DIARY

INTELLIGENCE SUMMARY.
(Erase heading not required.)

Army Form C. 2118.

Place	Date	Hour	Summary of Events and Information	Remarks and references to Appendices
RONGY	1/8		2 Sections making Divisional Baths House in RONGY. 17.d.9.9.(Sheet 44.)	
	"		" " " " " in RONGY Wood.	
	"	½	" Launching 2 rafts on ESCAUT River at D.20.c.0.8. (Sheet 44) Lieut. H.G.Redgrave in charge, at night.	PPR
do	2/8		½ Section Stand-by for bridging.	
			1 Sec. on Bath house RONGY.	
do.	3/8	1	" making rafts at Bn.H.Q. BLEHARIES	PPR
		1	" erecting Gas-Curtains at do. do.	
		1	" Stands-by for bridging.	
		1	" making wire cables for rafts.	
		1½	" on Bath-house RONGY.	PPR
		1½	" at BLEHARIES making 21 Rafts at Bn.H.Q.	
do	7/8	2½	" do do 31 Catamaran rafts.	PPR
		2½	" on Bath-house RONGY. completed.	
		5/2	" making wire cables for rafts.	
		5/2	" Carrying Catamaran-rafts from Bn.H.Q. to C.H.Q. BLEHARIES at night.	PPR
		5/2	" Testing rafts at RONGY.	
do	5/8		3 Sections making rafts at Bn.H.Q. BLEHARIES.	
		1	" Stands-by for bridging	PPR
do.	6/8	1	" testing pattern rafts in Chateau Moat RONGY for 175 Inf. Bde.	PPR
	7/8	2	" making rafts at Bn.H.Q. BLEHARIES.	PPR
		1	" Stands - by for bridging.	

WAR DIARY
INTELLIGENCE SUMMARY.
(Erase heading not required.)

Army Form C. 2118.

Place	Date	Hour	Summary of Events and Information	Remarks and references to Appendices
RONGY	7/8		1 Sec: testing rafts on Chateau Moat. RONGY. For demonstration before Corps Commdr & G.O.C. Divn:	PME
			2 Sec: making rafts at Bn. HQ. BLEHARIES.	
			1 " Sec: Gas Curtains at do.	
	8/8	9hrs	1 Sec: launching 10 Barrel Catamaran Raft on ESCAUT FLEUVE at ESPAIN. Trying tow lines across river & ferrying loading companies & Inf: over same in pursuit of Enemy. Also launching Barrel-pier Bridge for Pack Mules at D.26.a.1.7. (Sheet 44) under 2 Lieut F. PRIDE. 2 ORs wounded during operations.	
		11hrs	1 Sec: bridging 2 Culverts in main road at D.26.a. & felling trees for road boxes & clearing road of debris under Lieut N.F. TREFY.	
		17.45hrs		
		17.15hrs	2 Sec: Throwing across pontoon bridge at ESPAIN. D.25.b.9.5 making approach road on West Bank. Bridge consisted of 1 Service Trestle & 5 Pontoons under Lieut H.G. PEARSE.	PME
			The above operations were completed at 20.30hrs ready for the Forces.	
			Transport Field Sers.	
			Wounded men: 506577 Cpl: GOUGH. A.M.	
			506582 Sppr: DASH. H.G.	

Army Form C. 2118.

WAR DIARY

~~INTELLIGENCE SUMMARY~~

(Erase heading not required.)

Instructions regarding War Diaries and Intelligence Summaries are contained in F. S. Regs., Part II. and the Staff Manual respectively. Title pages will be prepared in manuscript.

Place	Date	Hour	Summary of Events and Information	Remarks and references to Appendices
TONGY.	9/4/18	8 hrs	Co. moves to BLEHARIES and prepares for forming heavy pontoon Bridge at ESPAIN. ("Type D") for Motor Transport, hauling timber from MAULDE dump for above purpose, improving approach road to medium bridge fixed on previous day & generally assisting divisional transport across river. New pontoons brought up by M.T. from I. Corps to BLEHARIES.	PR
	9/4/18	12 hrs	No.3 Sec. under 2nd Lt. A. TREBY moves to BLEHARIES & are off loaded by 503 F.M. Cy. R.E. Vehicles returned.	PR
BLEHARIES.	10/4/18		Co. moves to WIERS, repairing road through ROEULX – LEGIS – ROUILLON – WIERS en route. 7 Craters filled, 2 Culverts bridged. No.2 Sec. is relieved at MAULDE by 290 A.T. Co who also taken charge of ESPAIN Bridge-head.	PR
WIERS.	11/4/18	8 hrs	Co moves to BELOEIL, carrying out road repairs en-route. All four Sections commence work for construction of Heavy Bridge at B.3.d.9.5. (Sheet 45)	PR
BELOEIL	12/4/18		All Co. on Heavy Bridging (Trestle) at B.3.d.9.5. ditto	PR
do.	13/4/18		All ditto. 2nd Lieut. F. L. SPAIN. reporting units after Service Leave to U.K.	PR

Army Form C. 2118.

WAR DIARY

INTELLIGENCE SUMMARY.

(Erase heading not required.)

Instructions regarding War Diaries and Intelligence Summaries are contained in F. S. Regs., Part II. and the Staff Manual respectively. Title pages will be prepared in manuscript.

Place	Date	Hour	Summary of Events and Information	Remarks and references to Appendices
BELOEIL	14/11/18		3 Sections on Heavy Trestle Bridge at B.3.d.9.5. (Sheet 75)	
"			1 " on Cleaning vehicles & Co. Stores +c.	
"	15/11/18		As for 14th	
"	16/11/18		# Sec: erecting Divisional Baths at BELOEIL.	
			# " " " " BASCLES.	
			1/5 " Cleaning vehicles, checking stores +c.	
			2 " on Heavy Trestle Bridge at B.3.d.9.5. Decking roadway completed for Mn Arties load traffic.	
"	17/11/18		# Sec: on Baths at BELOEIL.	
			# " " " " BASCLES. (completed)	
			1 " Fixing hand-rails on Trestle Bridge B.3.d.9.5.	
			Remainder of Co on Church Parades. Thanksgiving Services.	
"	18/11/18		# Sec: on Baths at BELOEIL.	
			1 " Clearing up Bridge site at B.3.d.9.5. completing over trestle	
			Remainder, fetching Pontoon equipment from BLEHARIES, clearing vehicles & checking stores	
"	19/11/18		1 Sec: Clearing up surplus stores on Bridge site B.3.d.9.5. furniture toward +c.	
			# " on Baths at BELOEIL (completed)	
			Remainder inspected by O.R.E. also inspection St. G. Billets	
			Lieut. H.C. PEARCE also on Special Leave to U.K.	

Lieut. H.C. PEARCE

Army Form C. 2118.

WAR DIARY
INTELLIGENCE SUMMARY.
(Erase heading not required.)

Instructions regarding War Diaries and Intelligence Summaries are contained in F. S. Regs., Part II. and the Staff Manual respectively. Title pages will be prepared in manuscript.

Place	Date	Hour	Summary of Events and Information	Remarks and references to Appendices
BELOEIL	20/8		1 Sec: Clearing Bridge Site at B.3.d.9.5.	PhP
"	21/8		2 " digging up sleepers from BELOEIL Station Yard for Bridging at U.21.6.7.0.	PhP
			No 3 Sec: under Lieut. N.H. TREFY. moves to WAUDIGNIES + commences bridging at U.21.6.7.0.	
"			1 Sec: Bridging at U.21.6.7.0.	PhP
			2 " Recovering Sleepers from BELOEIL Stn. Yard for bridge at U.21.6.7.0	PhP
"	22/8		1st Lieut. J.F. FISHMAN reports for reinforcement from R.E. Depôt.	PhP
			1st Sec: Bridging at U.21.6.7.0.	
			3 " Batting Pit Inspection.	PhP
"	23/8		1 " Bridging at U.21.6.7.0.	
			3 " Squad Drill.	
"	27/8		1 " Completing Bridge at U.21.6.7.0. Returns from WAUDIGNIES to BELOEIL in Charge of Lieut. N.H. Treffy.	PhP
"	25/8		3 " Church Parade.	PhP
	26/8		" " Coy Training + Recreation.	PhP
	27/8		" " do.	PhP
	28/8		" " do.	PhP
	29/8		" " do. 2nd Lieut J.F. DAVIS is struck off strength of Unity Authority A.G.I Branch 55/584710. M.I.D.28	PhP
WEIRS	30/8		Coy moves to WEIRS.	PhP
			Coy employed on reconnoitring Billets.	

O.C. 504th FD. COY. R.E.

WAR DIARY

INTELLIGENCE SUMMARY.

504TH FD. COY. R.E.

Army Form C. 2118.

Place	Date	Hour	Summary of Events and Information	Remarks and references to Appendices
WIERS.	1/12/18		Church Parade in morning. Recreation in afternoon. Lt. G.R. CONNOR with 2 G.O.R. details from 113 Inf. Bde. Group reports for Trades Training. Coy Fatigues, cleaning transport &c.	
"	2		Do for 2nd inst.	
"	3		1 N.C.O. + 5 Sappers to GRANGUES to work at Divisional Baths. Remainder of Coy. on billets, coy. ground fatigues.	
"	4		R.E. Services with 113 Inf. Bde.	
"	5		No. 1 + 2 Sections ind. out/vest valuours and H'vest grain more to TRENCHES for HONNUN + AVCURDO.	
			No. 3 Sn. Sections on Coy. Fatigues, cookhouses &C.	
			58th FD. Co. No. 1234 dated 11/6 to No. 506471 Sper. (A/cpl.) H.G. GOLDING. Awarded M.M.	
			Do. No. 1276 dated 15/11 " No. 408302 " G. BREWSTER " M.M.	
			58th FD. No. No. 1276 dated 15/11 " 2/Lieut. T. PRIDE, R.E. " M.C.	
			58th " " 11. 1274 " No. 506471 2nd Cpl. A. TUCKER " M.M.	
			" Do. 1239 " 2/8 " 506557 Cpl. A.M. GOUGH " M.M.	
			Work do. 1239 5.12.18 and 2 Lieut. (A/Major) W.H. TAMLYN " M.C.	
"	6		Ditto	
"	7		Ditto	
"	8		Church Parade.	
"	9		Work as on 5th inst. + hauling R.E. Materials from HAULVE dumps.	
"	10			

Army Form C. 2118.

WAR DIARY
INTELLIGENCE SUMMARY.
(Erase heading not required.)

504TH FD. COY. R.E.

Instructions regarding War Diaries and Intelligence Summaries are contained in F.S. Regs., Part II. and the Staff Manual respectively. Title pages will be prepared in manuscript.

Place	Date	Hour	Summary of Events and Information	Remarks and references to Appendices
WIERS.	11/12/18		2 Secs: on R.E. Services for 113 Inf.Bde. at BASECLES	
"	12		2 " Coy. fatigues and loading R.E. materials from MAULDE dump.	
"			2 " at BASECLES.	
"	13		2 " on Coy. fatigues and loading party at Bat. R.E. Dump, WIERS.	
"			2 " at BASECLES	
"	14		Remainder of Coy. Bathing Parade.	
"			Do. for 12th inst.	
"	15		Church Parade.	
"	16		2 Secs. at BASECLES.	
"			2 " on Coy. fatigues & fitting up Recreation Hall.	
"	17		Do. for 16th inst.	
"	18		Do. for 16th inst.	
"	19		Do. for 16th inst.	
"	20		2 Secs: repairing Coy. from BASECLES.	
"			2 " on B. fatigues, fitting up Recreation Hall, Public latrines, Repairs to WIERS Bridge.	
"	21		All Coy. fitting up new floors for No. 1 & 2 Sections, fitting up Recreation Hall, Public latrines, repairs to WIERS Bridge.	

WAR DIARY

INTELLIGENCE SUMMARY

504TH FD. COY. R.E.

Army Form C. 2118.

Place	Date	Hour	Summary of Events and Information	Remarks and references to Appendices
WIERS.	22/12		Church Parade. Honours & Awards. 58th Divn: T.R.O. 1283 dated 19/12 Lieut N.H. TRERY. R.E. awarded M.C.	PRP
"	23.		Company parties hauling bricks, making Public & Section Latrines, Fitting up Recreation Hall, Mess Rooms for Nos 1 & 2 Sections.	PRP
"	24.		Company parties making latrines, fitting up Recreation Hall, Mess Rooms. Detach.t Lt Funen from 173 Inf Bde: return to units for Xmas.	PRP
"	25.		Church Parade in Morning. Coy Xmas Dinner in afternoon.	PRP
"	26.		Boxing Day. Football recreation.	PRP
"	27.		Coy Parade for completing Demobilization Forms. 1/23 Duf. Bde: Detachment rejoins	PRP
"	28.		As for 27th	PRP
"	29.		Church Parade	PRP
"	30.		1 Sapper Sergt, 9 o.r. proceed on detachment to BASECLES to supervise 173 Inf: Bde in constructing Rifle Range & Incinerator. Section on repairs to main road bridge WIERS. 1 " " constructing trestle road bridge at K.11.a.4.8 (Sheet 74E) Remainder on Coy: fatigues	PRP
"	31		1 Sapper Sergt, 12 o.r. proceed on detachment to QUEVAUCAMPS to work for Division. Remainder as for 30th	PRP

PHILPS, Major
O.C. 504TH FD. COY. R.E.

504 2d Cay RL
VA 25

Stan

11

Army Form C. 2118.

WAR DIARY
INTELLIGENCE SUMMARY.

504TH FD. COY. R.E.

(Erase heading not required.)

Place	Date	Hour	Summary of Events and Information	Remarks and references to Appendices
WIERS.	1919 Jany 1st		Detachment 1 Sergt: 12.O.R. at QUEVELCAMPS making Tournament Ground for 58th Div:	PNR
	2nd		" 1 " 9.O.R. " BASECLES making Rifle Range for 173 Inf: Bde: and making Incinerator for Town Major.	PNR PNR PNR
	3		1 Section on Repairs to main road Bridge in WIERS K.4. & I.II (Sheet 44) K.II.d.4.8 do.	
	4		1 Remainder on hauling materials & Cy. fatigues, making latrines, Cookhouses for Settees.	
	5		As for 1st inst.	PNR
	6		" " " "	PNR PNR
do.			Church Parade	
do.			As for 1st inst.	
do.			1 N.C.O & 2 O.R. on detachment to BASECLES to erect New Shower Bath Apparatus in lieu of old apparatus.	PNR
do.			1 N.C.O. & 7 O.R. report to Camp Commdt: PERUWELZ for Sunday R.E. Services. Daily.	PNR PNR
do.	7.		As for 6th " " "	
do.	8.		" " "	
do.	9.		As for 6th "	
do.	10		As for 1st inst. 1 N.C.O. & 2 O.R. return from detachment at BASECLES.	PNR
do	11		1 Lieut F.PRIDE proceeds on Service Leave to U.K. 3	PNR

Army Form C. 2118.

WAR DIARY
or
INTELLIGENCE SUMMARY.

(Erase heading not required.)

504TH FD. COY. R.E.

Instructions regarding War Diaries and Intelligence Summaries are contained in F. S. Regs., Part II. and the Staff Manual respectively. Title pages will be prepared in manuscript.

Place	Date	Hour	Summary of Events and Information	Remarks and references to Appendices
VIERS.	12th		Church Parade.	
do.	13th		As for 15th inst.	
do.	14th		Ditto	
do.	15th		Ditto	
do.	16th		Ditto	
do.	17th		Ditto	
			Major R. RON proceeds on Service Leave to U.K. and hands over Command of Unit to Capt. H. L. BAZALGETTE.	
do.	18th		Bathing Parade.	
do.	19th		Church Parade.	
do.	20th		As for 1st inst. Party of 1 NCO and 13 ORs proceed to I.O.K. for the purpose of Reconnaissance.	
do.	21st		Additional party of 1 NCO & 11 ORs proceed to QUESNOY-CAMPS to assist in preparation of Tournament (Boxing). Trestle Bridge at R.11.A.4.8. handed over to 511 Field Coy. R.E. Other work as for 17th inst.	

Army Form C. 2118.

WAR DIARY
or
INTELLIGENCE SUMMARY. 504TH FD. COY. R.E.

(Erase heading not required.)

Instructions regarding War Diaries and Intelligence Summaries are contained in F. S. Regs., Part II. and the Staff Manual respectively. Title pages will be prepared in manuscript.

Place	Date	Hour	Summary of Events and Information	Remarks and references to Appendices
WIERS	22/9		Attachment of 1 Capt: 23 O.R. at OUSVAUCAMPS preparing Tournament Ground for 56th Divn. Detachment 1 Comp. 110R at PASSELLES making Effets Kays for 173 Inf. Bde. Section in Repair Train Accidents in WIERS K4 b 11 (Sheet 44) Repairing material paid by Railways S.E. Runners from WIERS to U.K. sent hand. Capt. H.L. BAZALGETTE proceed on leave to U.K. Over Command of Unit to Lieut. H.G. PEARSE.	A.
"	23/9		Works as on 22nd inst.	H.S.P.
"	24/9		Ditto	H.S.P.
"	25/9		Ditto	
"	26/9		Church Parade. 8 N.C.O. 8 O.R.	H.S.P.
"	27/9		Work as on 22nd inst.	H.S.P.
"	28/9		5 N.C.O. 7 O.R. proceed to U.K. for demobilisation. Work as on 22nd inst, except work on body of men at WIERS K4 b11 (Sheet 44) suspended. Work as on 28 th inst	H.S.P.
"	29/9		Ditto	H.S.P.
"	30/9		Ditto	H.S.P.
"	31/9		I Lieut. F. PRIDE returned from leave home & U.K.	H.S.P.

N. G. ......
O.C. 504TH FD. COY. R.E.

Army Form C. 2118.

WAR DIARY
INTELLIGENCE SUMMARY
(Erase heading not required.)

Place	Date	Hour	Summary of Events and Information	Remarks and references to Appendices
WIERS	1/2/19		Attachment of 1 Sergt 7 O.R. at BASECLES making Rifle Range and Latreeny Covers for 173 Inf Brigade	APP
	2/2/19		Attachment of 1 Sergt 11 O.R. at QUEVAUCAMPS making Surround to mount Guard. 2 O.R. proceeded on Demobilyation. Strength reported 580 38 O.R. proceeded on Demobilyation	APP
	3/2/19		Church Parade. Work as on 1 st. 3 O.R. proceeded on Demobilyation, & N.H.7 ERRY Ponsen Rank & U.K.	APP
	4/2/19		— do —	APP
	5/2/19		— do —	APP
	6/2/19		Attachment withdrawn from QUEVAUCAMPS on completion of work. Other work as on 1 st inst	APP
	7/2/19		Work as on 6 th inst. 2/Lt F PRIDE and 5 O.R. proceeded on Demobilyation	APP
	8/2/19		— do —	APP
	9/2/19		Church Parade. 3 N.C.O. 1 O.R. proceeded on Demobilyation	APP
	10/2/19		Work as on 6 th inst. 15 O.R. to credit on Demobilyation	APP
	11/2/19		— do — Major R Row returned from Sich Leave U.K. and took over Com	APP
	12/2/19		Attachment withdrawn from BASECLES	APP
	13/2/19		7 O.R. proceeded on Demobilyation. Remainder on Coy duties.	APP
	14		Coy duties	APP
	15			APP

WAR DIARY

INTELLIGENCE SUMMARY.
(Erase heading not required.)

Army Form C. 2118.

Place	Date	Hour	Summary of Events and Information	Remarks and references to Appendices
WIETS.	16/2/19		Church Parade & Coy. Duties.	
	17		Coy. Duties	
	18		Do.	
	19		Do.	
	20		Do.	
	21		Do.	
	22		Coy. moves to LEUZE in accordance with C.R.E. 53rd Divn.; Order No 76 All.20/2	
LEUZE	23		Fitting up billets & stables &c	
	24		Ditto	
			Lieut. N.H. TRERY proceeded on Demobilization	
			1/Lieut. H.L. LISHMAN " " Service Leave (14 days) to U.K.	
	25		Coy. duties.	
	26		Ditto	
	27		Ditto. Capt. H.L. BAZALGETTE returned from Leave to U.K. & take Command of 503 Fd.Cg.R.E. in accordance with C.R.E. 53rd Divn. T.O. No.99 All.37/2 (Authority A.B. 55/6885 (O) All.13/2)	
	28		Ditto. 2nd Lieut. J.L. LISHMAN is posted to 503 Field Cy.R.E. with effect from 6/2	
	28		Coy. Duties. in accordance with C.R.E. 2 56th Divn. R.O. 103 All. 28/2 (Authority 58/Divn/2 Dec. No.D.273 All.27/2)	

P.P.Wr. Major
O.C. 504th FD. COY. R.E.

WAR DIARY
INTELLIGENCE SUMMARY

504TH FD. COY. R.E.

Army Form C. 2118.

Place	Date	Hour	Summary of Events and Information	Remarks and references to Appendices
LEUZE	March 1-1919 2/19		Coy. Duties.	
	3		Ditto. 2 Lieut. F.L. SPAIN proceeds on Special leave to U.K.	
	4		Coy. Duties. Instruction received for Unit to receive from Cadre "B" to "Queue B" authority. C.R.E. 58th Divn. No.E.P. 3/1. A.M. 37/19 & 58th Divn. No.D.S.7. A.M. 2/19	
	5		Coy. Duties.	
	6		Ditto.	
			Ditto. 14 O.R. posted to 23rd Field Coy. R.E. 1st Divn. in accordance with 2. R.E. 58th Divn. R.O. No.107 A.O 6/19. 10 O.R. proceed to join 23rd Fld. Coy. R.E. 4 " on leave in U.K.	
	7			
	8		Coy. Duties. Lieut. H.G. PEARSE proceeds to U.K. on Duty to report to W.O. in accordance with Final Army No. 1125/5168 A.Q.G. 28/19 and 58th Divn. No.76/6883	
	9		Coy. Duties. 10 O.R. proceeds to U.K. for Demobilization	
	10		Church Parade.	
	11		Coy. Duties. & checking equipment	
	12		Ditto.	
	13		Ditto.	
	14		Ditto.	
	15		Ditto.	
	16		Church Parade. One O.R. proceeds to U.K. for Demobilization	

Army Form C. 2118.

WAR DIARY
INTELLIGENCE SUMMARY
(Erase heading not required.)

504TH FD. COY. R.E.

Place	Date	Hour	Summary of Events and Information	Remarks and references to Appendices
LEUZE	17/3/19		Coy duties + Acting Coy Commander - 2/Lieut. F.L. Spain deputises (Company Commander) whilst on leave to U.K. 16-3-19. Authority A.G. 55/715(O) of 17-3-1919	DMC
	18/3/19		Work as for 17-3-19 - 2/Lieut. J.L. Lishman 503rd Field Coy. R.E. was posted to this unit to complete CADRE "A" establishment - Authority - 58th Div. A/6/71.35 of 20-3-19.	DMC
	19/3/19		Work as for 18-3-19	DMC
	20/3/19		Coy duties + Cleaning Vehicles	DMC
	21/3/19		ditto	DMC
	22/3/19		ditto	DMC
	23/3/19		Church Parade -	DMC
	24/3/19		Coy duties + Cleaning Vehicles (Morning Call)	DMC
	25/3/19		ditto - MAJOR R. RON takes over command of 504 D.W.T. R.E. (Field Coys.) Vice Lt.Col. A.J. SAVAGE. D.S.O. R.E. Authy 58th D/S R.O. No 776 of 26-3-19	
	26/3/19		ditto	
	27/3/19		ditto	DMC

Army Form C. 2118.

WAR DIARY
INTELLIGENCE SUMMARY. 504TH FD. COY. R.E.
(Erase heading not required.)

Instructions regarding War Diaries and Intelligence Summaries are contained in F.S. Regs., Part II. and the Staff Manual respectively. Title pages will be prepared in manuscript.

Place	Date	Hour	Summary of Events and Information	Remarks and references to Appendices
LEUZE	Mar 28/19		Coy Duties & Recreation. Route March	
	29/19		Coy Duties - Rifle & Billet Inspection	
	30/19		Church Parade	
	31/19		Coy Duties and Coal American Fatigue	

31 - 3 - 1919.

P.S. Major, R.E. (T.)
O.C. 504TH FD. COY. R.E.

WAR DIARY or INTELLIGENCE SUMMARY

504TH FD. COY. R.E.

Army Form C. 2118.

Place	Date	Hour	Summary of Events and Information	Remarks and references to Appendices
LEUZE	1st April 19		Coy. duties + Physical Exercises (Morning Only)	
	2nd		do + Rubbing softball games	
	3rd		do + Route March + Bathing Parade	
	4th		do + Fatigues	
	5th		do +	
	6th		do + Rougby suits	
	7th		Church Parade -	
	8th		Coy duties + Painting vehicles + Bathing Parade	
	9th		do , do , do	
	10th		do , do , do	
	11th		do , do , do	
	12th		Rifle + Army Corps Inspection	
	13th		Church Parade	
	14th		Dismantling German interment GRANDGLISE + Bathing Parade	
	15th		do do	

Army Form C. 2118.

WAR DIARY
or
INTELLIGENCE SUMMARY.

504TH FD. COY. R.E.

(Erase heading not required.)

Place	Date	Hour	Summary of Events and Information	Remarks and references to Appendices
LEUZE	1919 April 16th		Instructing German citizens GRANDGLISE —	
	17th		do do do Major R. Rao	
			Handing over command of Company to 1st Lieut T. Lakshman	
			and proceeds to B.R. for demobilization	
	18th		Good Friday – Holiday	
	19th		Instructing Germans citizens GRANDGLISE - contd.	
	20th		Church Parade	
	21st		Coy. Sports.	
	22nd		do do	
	23rd		Coy. Fatigues, cleaning & returning vehicles, Regtl. F&B Work M.T. taking over command of Company vice 1st Lieut J.K. LISHMAN (Authority) from 22/4/1919 & 58th Divl. Schl. Group - VI D.B.G. 1388 dated 26/4/1919)	
	24.		Coy Fatigues, cleaning & returning vehicles.	
	25.		do do	

Army Form C. 2118.

WAR DIARY
~~INTELLIGENCE~~ SUMMARY.

(Erase heading not required.)

504TH FD. COY. R.E.

Instructions regarding War Diaries and Intelligence Summaries are contained in F. S. Regs., Part II. and the Staff Manual respectively. Title pages will be prepared in manuscript.

Place	Date	Hour	Summary of Events and Information	Remarks and references to Appendices
LEUZE	26 April 1919		Coy. Fatigues.	N.P.W
	27 "		Church Parade	N.P.W
	28 "		Coy Fatigues	N.P.W
	29 "		do	N.P.W
	30 "		Bathing Parade, work on Div. Reserve Supply Store.	N.P.W

O.C. 504TH FD. COY. R.E.

WAR DIARY

INTELLIGENCE SUMMARY.

(Erase heading not required.)

Army Form C. 2118.

Place	Date	Hour	Summary of Events and Information	Remarks and references to Appendices
LEUZE	May 1st 1919		Coy. Fatigues & Physical Training.	9pm
	2nd		Coy. Fatigues & Physical Training.	9pm
	3rd		Coy. Fatigues & Physical Training.	9pm
	4th		Church Parade	9pm
	5th		Coal Fatigue.	9pm
	6th		Coy. Fatigue	9pm
	7th		Route March	9pm
	8th		Bathing Parade day duties	9pm
	9th		Physical Training	9pm
	10th		Coy. Fatigues	9pm
	11th		Church Parade	9pm
	12th		General Fatigues overhauling Tool Carts	9pm
	13th		do do do	9pm
	14th		Coy. Fatigues & Pay Parade	9pm

WAR DIARY

Army Form C. 2118.

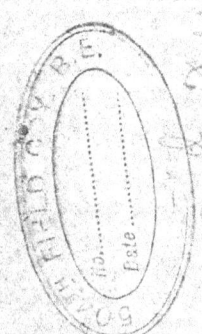

Place	Date	Hour	Summary of Events and Information	Remarks and references to Appendices
LEUZE	May 1919 14th		Bathing Parade - 5 Men proceeded to MONS for demobilisation	9P.M.
	15th		Repairs to roofs as tank Store bump - Coy Fatigues	9P.M.
	16th		Coy Fatigues	9P.M.
	17th		Muster Parade (Sunday)	9P.M.
	18th		Coy Fatigues	9P.M.
	19th		do - 5 Men to MONS for demobilisation	
	20th		Soccer 8 J Coy 2 Officers 40 ORs (Football Carnival Meeting)	
			58th R.G No. DG 1697 at 6 5.17 M)	9P.M.
	21st		Coy Fatigues	9P.M.
	22nd		Bathing Parade - NCO 150pm - Reg'l Police Duty	9P.M.
	23rd		Coy Fatigues - Pay Parade	
	24th		do	9P.M.
	25th		Muster Parade (Sunday)	9P.M.
	26th		Coy Fatigues + Reg'l Police Duty	9P.M.

Army Form C. 2118.

WAR DIARY

~~INTELLIGENCE SUMMARY~~

(Erase heading not required.)

Instructions regarding War Diaries and Intelligence Summaries are contained in F. S. Regs., Part II. and the Staff Manual respectively. Title pages will be prepared in manuscript.

Place	Date	Hour	Summary of Events and Information	Remarks and references to Appendices
LEUZE	May 27th 1919		Coy. Fatigues	9.P.W
	28th		Physical Training. - 1 N.C.O. for Bn' Equipment Store Guard	9.P.W
	29th		Bathing Parade.	9.P.W
	30th		Coy. Fatigues.	9.P.W
	31st		do. do.	9.P.W

G.P. White Lieut. R.E.
O.C. 504TH FD. COY. R.E.

O.C. R.E. Records.
G.H.Q.
British Armies in France

Herewith copy of War
Diary (504 Field Co R.E.)
for the undermentioned period
1st June 1919 to 20 June 1919

[signature] R.E.
O.C. 504 Field Co R.E.

20/6/19

504 (Fd) Co. R.E.

Army Form C. 2118.

WAR DIARY
or
INTELLIGENCE SUMMARY.
(Erase heading not required.)

Instructions regarding War Diaries and Intelligence Summaries are contained in F. S. Regs., Part II. and the Staff Manual respectively. Title pages will be prepared in manuscript.

Place	Date	Hour	Summary of Events and Information	Remarks and references to Appendices
LEUZE	June 1st 1919.		Church Parade.	J.R.W
	2nd		Coy. Fatigues.	J.R.W
	3rd		do. - 2 men repairing tools Equipment Store	J.R.W
	4th		Guard Room —	J.R.W
	5th		Coy. duties.	J.R.W
	6th		Coy. duties	J.R.W
	7th		Draft of 27 ORs proceeded to MONS for demobilisation. Leaving 1 Officer & 13 ORs w EQUIPMENT GUARD.	J.R.W
	8th		Coy. duties.	J.R.W
	9th		LIEUT. E.A.T. BILHAM returned from U.K. Took over 813. Command of Company vice LIEUT. F.C.B. WILLS M.C. oo from 5th June.— Ref./C.R.E. 58th Div Group R.O. 189 d/d 4/6/19 June/19 (Authority D.G. R.O. No 909 d/d 4th June/19.	813.
	10th		Coy duties,	

D. D. & L., London, E.C.
(A8001) Wt. W1771/M2031 750,000 5/17. Sch. 52 Forms/C2118/14

WAR DIARY
INTELLIGENCE SUMMARY
(Erase heading not required.)

Army Form C. 2118.

Place	Date	Hour	Summary of Events and Information	Remarks and references to Appendices
LEUZE	June 11th 1919		Coy. Butler.	E.B.
	12th		Lt. Wills resumed command of Coy. vice Lt. E.A.J. Bilham	R.W.
			Coy. preparing vehicles for entrainment.	G.R.W.
	13th		Coy. Entrains for ANTWERP	G.R.W.
ANTWERP	14th		Coy. arrives ANTWERP. Vehicles parked.	G.R.W.
"	15th		In Camp. Snipers & fatigues.	G.R.W.
"	16th		Entrained for Boulogne.	G.R.W.
BOULOGNE	17th		Arrive BOULOGNE, move on to large, after loading equipment	G.R.W.
"	18th		moved to Mulberough Camp	G.R.W.
"	19th		In Camp	G.R.W.
"	20th		Endeavour for England as Crew for launch	G.R.W.
			Wills died R.E.	G.R.W.

www.ingramcontent.com/pod-product-compliance
Lightning Source LLC
Chambersburg PA
CBHW081356160426
43192CB00013B/2423